Advance Praise for *Black School White School*

"In *Black School White School*, Jeffrey Brooks illuminates an understudied aspect of institutional racism in education: racism and racial privilege among educational leaders (such as principals). Brooks convincingly shows how White privilege and unconscious bias trickles down from administrators to teachers to, ultimately, infect the student body. After reading this important book, one is thoroughly convinced that 'leadership matters' with respect to race and education."

—Dalton Conley, University Professor of the Social Sciences,
Chair of the Department of Sociology at New York University,
and author of *Honky* and *Being Black, Living in the Red*

"Brooks provides a much-needed empirical analysis of how race and culture function in schools. A must-read for both school leaders and those who prepare them."

—Sonya Douglass Horsford, University of Nevada, Las Vegas and author of
Learning in a Burning House: Educational Inequality, Ideology, and (Dis)Integration

"Powerful empirical insights on one of the most critical and knotty issues in school leadership today, by one of the profession's major postmodern scholars."

—Joseph F. Murphy, Vanderbilt University and author of
The Educator's Handbook for Understanding and Closing Achievement Gaps

"As one of our most thoughtful leadership scholars, Jeff Brooks digs into race, leadership, and schools. This book carefully and openly tackles a vital intersection of racism and educational leadership that for too long school administrators have turned a blind eye. If we are serious about creating equitable and excellent schools, Brooks' account in *Black School White School* offers a poignant and important look at these very real issues. This gritty account and sharp analysis depicts the realities of racism that are perpetuated across schools in the United States, but leaves us with a sense that this can change—that school leaders are a powerful leverage point in addressing race and educational racism."

—George Theoharis, Syracuse University
and author of *The School Leaders Our Children Deserve*

"Once again Jeff Brooks brings a finely tuned eye and mind to the matter of race, race relations, and educational practice in the schools with *Black School White School*. Anyone who thought they knew about race and race relations in the schools will find in this volume new content and highly nuanced descriptions not available anywhere else. This is patient and persistent research of a microcosm writ large in our society."

—Fenwick W. English, University of North Carolina at Chapel Hill,
author of *Theory in Educational Administration*,
and editor of *The Sage Handbook of Educational Leadership*

"A sensitive, insightful, and compelling investigation of race in our schools. Dr. Brooks' book is a seminal work on this topic and a must-read for all educators."

—Jacqueline Stefkovich, Professor, Educational Leadership & Policy Studies, The Pennsylvania State University, and co-author of *Ethical Leadership and Decision Making in Education: Applying Theoretical Perspectives to Complex Dilemmas*

"This is a book that needed to be written, and a story that anyone claiming to be interested in education leadership must read. We know that race and race relations in schools influence and are influenced by what leaders do, but rarely have I seen this expressed so clearly in the words of those live it."

—David Allan Walker, Chinese University of Hong Kong and author of *School Leadership and Management: Adopting a Cultural Perspective*

"This book brings to bare the nuances of racism and leadership in the K–12 context and is based on seminal research that sensitizes our field to more deeply examine the enduring nature of racism. It also reminds us that the struggle for social justice continues."

—Gaetane Jean-Marie, University of Oklahoma and co-editor of *Women of Color in Higher Education: Turbulent Past, Promising Future*

"*Black School White School* is an exciting and much-needed discussion for the field of Educational Leadership. Jeff Brooks has a 'no holds barred' exposition of a very touchy subject for many. He has managed to gently yet firmly tackle this topic and open the door for greater discussion. This is a must-read for anyone working in or interested in education."

—Judy A. Alston, Ashland University and co-editor of *Herstories: Leading with the Lessons of the Lives of Black Women Activists*

"Brooks' rigorous and thoughtful conceptual and empirical analysis exposes the inadequacies and indeed the dangers of educators, academics, and policymakers continuing to view educational leadership as a color-blind enterprise. The clear, insightful voices of students, educators, and others that Brooks persuasively presents to us unequivocally remind us that a post-racialized educational system has not yet been realized and that we as educators—both in schools and in preparation programs—have much work still to do."

—Gary Crow, Indiana University and co-author of *The Principalship: New Roles in a Professional Learning Community*

"Finally, a book that grapples, honestly and critically, with the 'fourth R' in education: Racism. In an era discursively constructed as 'post-racial' and 'color-blind,' Brooks' *Black School White School* keeps one of the most important conversations of our time alive."

—David Brunsma, Virginia Tech University and co-editor of *Beyond Black: Biracial Identity in America*

"In *Black School White School*, Jeff Brooks uncovers the vexing complexities that confront students, teachers, and administrators when it comes to race, class, and perceived and actual privilege. He does all of this in an engaging and lively writing style that will keep the reader engrossed from beginning to end— something that is all too rare in scholarly works."

—Catherine A. Lugg, Rutgers University

"*Black School White School* examines the role that race and race relations continue to play in our public schools, and how divided our lives continue to be along racial lines. In a society that espouses to have moved 'beyond' racism with the election of an African American president, this book illustrates how racism is woven into the fabric of our society, as race and race relations continue to influence leadership practice, and ultimately the education of students. *Black School White School* provides a glimpse into the struggles that many urban high schools are experiencing in the 21st century, and adds to the much-needed research on social justice leadership."

—Sarah L. Diem, University of Missouri–Columbia

"In education there is often an unfortunate divide between theory and practice, between the Ivory Tower and the real world of schools. In *Black School White School*, Brooks invites the reader into both worlds with rich detail, profound insight, and compelling questions. I could not put this book down!"

—Lisa A. W. Kensler, Auburn University

"In a recent past, the preparation of professionals in educational leadership was limited to providing students with quality instruction and safe environments. Sorely missing from this preparation is any attention toward inequities in society. In the forefront of this movement we find scholars like Jeffrey Brooks, who in this volume piercingly addresses the indifference to race issues in the field of educational leadership, and awakens us from avoidance and apathy towards injustices that returns to the school environment in the form of recurrent silence. Brooks reminds us that the responsibility of impacting students' futures is not insular—it is in the active role of educators, educational leaders, and scholars in purposefully changing minds and hearts in order to contribute for a better society in America."

—Elizabeth (Betty) Murakami-Ramalho, University of Texas at San Antonio and co-editor of *Educational Leaders Encouraging the Intellectual and Professional Capacity of Others: A Social Justice Agenda*

"This book makes a unique contribution to the ongoing discussion on race and how it impacts school leadership. It skillfully blends real-world schooling experiences, a rigorous methodology, and potent theoretical insights. In an era when race is still rarely discussed, especially in educational leadership, it reminds us that racism still exists, racial issues are complicated, and race still matters."

—Floyd Beachum, Lehigh University and co-author of *Cultural Collision and Collusion: Reflections on Hip-Hop Culture, Values, and Schools*

"Through an engaging, narrative writing style, Jeff Brooks weaves theory and practice around the issues of educational inequity, race, and race relations, thus creating a remarkable piece of thought-provoking work that demonstrates how racism influences educational leadership. Of major significance are the ways in which Brooks identifies cultural and sub-cultural norms and beliefs around race and race relations, and then explores how these dynamics influence the kind of education students receive. *Black School White School: Racism and Educational (Mis) Leadership* has identity at the core of one's leadership. It will inspire students, practitioners, and scholars to think critically about our own practices and ways in which we all can promote and foster models of leadership that will address the racial, cultural, and ethnic makeup of school communities."

—Anthony H. Normore, California State University–Dominguez Hills
and editor of *Global Perspectives on Educational Leadership Reform: The Development
and Preparation of Leaders of Learning and Learners of Leadership*

"Polemic diatribes critiquing 'the achievement gap' and obtuse theories of how to ameliorate it are a dime a dozen. Scholarship digging into the nitty-gritty reality of race in school is rare, and precisely what is needed to inform educational leadership. Brooks delivers both a nuanced, intimate account of the messy, complicated, contradictory day-to-day world in the school and a cogent, thoughtful analysis of race and equity in education. *Black School White School* is a refreshingly candid, persuasive, and ultimately hopeful work to push the thinking of principals, superintendents, policymakers, and scholars in the field."

—Martin Scanlan, Marquette University

"This is an engagingly written and perceptive account of a deeply complex area of school life that profoundly affects the educational experience and life chances of students. The authors' analysis eschews simple interpretations. Rather, it surfaces the nuances and complexities through accessible and theoretically informed reflections by the authors on their encounters as researchers, taking the reader inside the everyday realities of race and race relations in U.S. schools."

—Philip A. Woods, University of Gloucestershire

"Dr. Brooks' book offers a balanced examination of issues of racism and the often complex and contextual dynamic of the intersection of race and leadership. This book offers critical perspectives not only for educational leadership but provides interdisciplinary implications for all of schooling."

—Noelle Witherspoon Arnold, University of Missouri–Columbia and editor of
Critical Perspectives on Spirituality, Religion, and African American Education

Black School
White School

RACISM AND EDUCATIONAL (MIS)LEADERSHIP

Jeffrey S. Brooks

Foreword by Lisa D. Delpit
Afterword by William Ayers

Teachers College
Columbia University
New York and London

The description of DuBois High School in Chapter 1 originally appeared in Brooks, J. S., Normore, A. H., Jean-Marie, G., & Hodgins, D. (2007). Distributed leadership for social justice: Influence and equity in an urban high school. *Journal of School Leadership, 17*(4), 378–408. Reprinted with the permission of the *Journal of School Leadership.*

Portions of Chapter 2 were previously published as the article Brooks, J. S., Normore, A. H., Jean-Marie, G., & Hodgins, D. (2007). Distributed leadership for social justice: Influence and equity in an urban high school. *Journal of School Leadership, 17*(4), 378–408. Reprinted with the permission of Rowman & Littlefield Publishing Group.

Portions of Chapter 3 were previously published as Brooks, J. S., & Jean-Marie, G. (2007). Black leadership, white leadership: Race and race relations in an urban high school. *Journal of Educational Administration, 45*(6), 756–768. Reprinted with permission of the Emerald Publishing Group Limited.

Portions of Chapter 9 were previously published in Brooks, J. S. (2007, Summer). Race and educational leadership: Conversation catalysts to prompt reflection, discussion, and action for individuals and organizations. *UCEA Review, XLVII*(2), 1–3. Reprinted with permission of UCEA.

Published by Teachers College Press, 1234 Amsterdam Avenue, New York, NY 10027

Library of Congress Cataloging-in-Publication Data

Brooks, Jeffrey S., 1970–
    Black school, White school : racism and educational (mis)leadership / Jeffrey S. Brooks ; Foreword by Lisa D. Delpit ; Afterword by William Ayers.
       pages cm
    Includes bibliographical references and index.
    ISBN 978-0-8077-5312-5 (pbk. : alk. paper)
      1. Racism in education—United States. 2. Educational leadership—United States. 3. African American school principals. I. Title.
    LC212.2.B76 2012
    370.89—dc23   2011047595

ISBN 978-0-8077-5312-5 (paper)

Printed on acid-free paper
Manufactured in the United States of America

19 18 17 16 15 14 13 12   8 7 6 5 4 3 2 1

Contents

Foreword: Educational Leadership:
It's Not About Race . . . Right? *by Lisa D. Delpit*   xi

Acknowledgments   xv

Introduction   1

1. Racism and Educational (Mis)Leadership in the United States   5

    Race in the United States   6

    Race and Education in the United States   7

    Mulholland Falls and DuBois High School:
    A Context to Study Racism and Educational Leadership   12

PART I: FROM SOCIAL JUSTICE TO RACISM

2. Distributed Leadership for Social Justice   17

    School Leadership: A Distributed Perspective   18

    Leadership for Social Justice:
    From Abstract Ideals to Everyday Practice   21

    Leaders as Transformational Public Intellectuals   21

    Leadership for Bridging and Connecting People   22

    School Leaders as Critical Activists   23

    Transformational Public Intellectualism,
    Stretched Across a School   24

    Distributed Anti-Intellectualism versus Liberation Leadership   24

International Baccalaureate Program:
One Subcommunity of Scholars for Social Justice   26

Black Leaders as Transformational Public Intellectuals   27

Bridgework as Distributed Leadership for Social Justice   28

Communication and Awareness:
Critical Aspects of Bridgework   28

Building Bridges for Social Justice:
Individual and Institutional Leadership   29

Distributed Critical Activism   30

Distributed *Conscientizacão*   30

Soft Revolutions and Hard Revolutions:
Activists Taking a Stand in Different Ways   32

Is Leadership for Social Justice Enough?   32

How Can Distributed Leadership
for Social Justice Improve Education?   35

3. **Black Leadership, White Leadership:
Race and Race Relations in an Urban High School**   37

School Leadership as a Racial Moiety   38

Black Leadership Subculture at DuBois High School   40

White Leadership Subculture at DuBois High School   42

Dual Culture Interaction at DuBois High School   45

PART II: RACISM AND EDUCATIONAL MISLEADERSHIP

4. **Honky Leadership: White Teacher in a Black School**   51

5. **The Black Leadership Experience:
Living the Dream or Expelled to Excel?**   61

Paul Alphonse, Guidance Counselor   61

Myra Watkins-Glenn, Social Studies Teacher   64

DeShawn Mooney, English Teacher   68

Paul Regis, Science Teacher 70

Good Teachers Are More Than Good Teachers 71

6. **That Program Ain't Never Done a Thing for Black Kids . . . or Has It?** 73

7. **The Silent Language of Racism** 89

The Silent Language 89

Interaction 91

Association 93

Subsistence 94

Sexuality 95

Territoriality 95

Temporality 96

Learning 97

Play 98

Defense 99

Conclusion 99

8. **Educational Misleadership** 101

Incompetence 101

Indifference and Apathy 104

Avoidance 106

Unethical Behavior 107

**PART III: LESSONS LEARNED
AND POSSIBILITIES FOR THE FUTURE**

9. **Moving Toward a New Educational Leadership** 115

Racism Influences Leadership Practice 115

Conclusion 124

Afterword: The Myth of a Post-Racial Society—
   A Conversation with Bill Ayers   125

Methodological Appendix   137
   Research Design   137
   Data Collection   137
   Data Analysis   138
   Validity   138

References   141

Index   149

About the Author   155

Educational Leadership: It's Not About Race . . . Right?

I notice an interesting phenomenon occurring along with having a Black president: a lot of people say that we don't have to talk about race or racism anymore. Thus, all of the issues emanating from right-wing politics, like those from the Tea Party, for example, supposedly have nothing to do with race. Yet, if a Martian arrived tomorrow to do an ethnography of the United States, it would be very clear that race is the subtext of all the conversations. This presents an interesting model that drifts into education as well as into every other factor of American life: Oh no, no, no, we are not talking issues of race, we are speaking about fair taxation, we are talking about economics, we're against socializing our political system, we are talking about *whatever else*. And so, we end up with individuals even acting against their own class interests—like poor White folks opposing universal health care—when what they are really responding to is issues of race.

In educational circles some of the "non-racial" policy decisions relate to who gets to teach. In city after city there is widespread removal or devaluing of Black teachers based on the belief that we can solve all our school problems by putting young, inexperienced, "better educated" White people in Black schools . . . but again, none of this relates to race. It seems policymakers just think these young people—with no commitment to be there for the long term, with insufficient training, with no experience with the population—are appropriate to teach poor African American children primarily because they are White. But it's not about race . . . Right?

I do want to be careful not to suggest that I think all people who come to schools through Teach for America or other short-term training programs are terrible—they're not. Some of them are wonderful. Many are very committed young people who are put in situations that are beyond their understanding. That said, some are only doing it for their resumes. I worry about these part-time saviors.

With our Black president, talking about race in education has ironically become more difficult than ever. If someone raises issues of race or racism, he or she is often accused of being a racist. It is not race, their detractors insist, it is poverty, single-parent homes, lack of motivation—all factors that are centered in the population itself rather than in what surrounds the children, like discriminatory policies, inadequate resources, inexperienced teachers, or a curriculum disconnected from the students' history or interests. It locates the problem in the students and their communities rather than in their schools. When that is the case, then there is nothing educators can do to solve the problem. Locating the problem outside of schools makes everything very convenient—it lets the schools off the hook for change. It's the families, or the communities or the students' native abilities. But it's not about racism . . . Right?

This construct deeply affects students' sense of self—we all define ourselves from the messages we get from our larger community about who we are. I once worked in a state that believed some purpose would be served by assigning all schools a letter grade. Miami Edison High School, located in a poor Haitian immigrant community, had been designated as a "triple F" or one year "quadruple F" school. The students were profoundly hurt by being identified with an institution that was described as such a failure in countless newspaper articles and television news reports. One young man said that being in an F school made him feel like an F person, that nobody thought there was anything good about him. Students easily become defeated in the face of attitudes that there is something wrong with them, that they'll never be good enough.

When young people believe that they are unable to do something or they believe they are less than others, they respond in one of two ways. Either they try to hide from the situation (those students who pull their hoods over their heads, put their heads on their desks, and try to become invisible). Or they act out during classroom instruction to interrupt lessons to try to prevent a situation that might prove them "less than." Thus, a lot of the hiding out and acting out we see in schools is a result of the students' internalization of the larger society's view of who they are.

I believe, like Jeff Brooks expresses in this book, that a large part of the problem in schools has to do with culture. I used to believe that the problem was solely one of the cultural mismatch between the school culture and the lived culture of the students in the school. The solution to that problem would be to understand the culture of the children of color and build pedagogy around it. But I have come to believe the real problem is not so much the culture of the children or the culture of the schools, but the culture of the larger American society. That is the culture that needs to be addressed. The larger society has consistently expressed a kind of cultural violence toward all things of African descent, and this national culture can crush children of color. We, as a country, desperately need to look at ourselves and use all of our collective energy to unravel belief systems that belittle any of our citizens.

In the educational arena, principals have a tremendous role to play in undoing racism and giving our young people the strength to persevere despite larger societal beliefs. Although I have usually worked with teachers and students, I have more recently had the opportunity to work with principals in a variety of settings. In one school with a predominantly African American student population, I was asked by a young Black principal to observe the classrooms and work with the teachers around creating culturally congruent pedagogical strategies. This principal had recently been appointed to the school. He was called in because the school was disorderly and the test scores were very low. Prior to his arrival there was a White female principal and a majority of White staff. I do not, however, believe that the race of the staff was the core problem, yet racialized attitudes played a large role in the school's difficulties. The problem was a belief system that held that these Black children could not be expected to excel academically or to act in a disciplined fashion. Expectations were low, instruction was weak, and rules and regulations were either nonexistent or unenforced. When the adults couldn't believe in the students' ability to excel, then the young people could not see themselves excelling.

The new principal set out to change the culture of the school. He hired more Black teachers, but he insisted that all staff, regardless of color, be held accountable for the academic excellence and the disciplined behavior of the students. He set out to counter the larger societal belief system that little could be expected of the Black children in the school. The curriculum of the school was not to be solely based on state tests, nor was it to be limited by textbooks. Teachers worked together during the school year and during the summer to develop curricular offerings in each subject area that were connected to the students' culture and their lives. As a part of their matriculation from 8th to 9th grade, each student developed a signature research project. I met a pair of 8th graders who were collaborating to create a video and written document on the history of jazz in Chicago. They researched printed information, interviewed musicians and music historians, created a soundtrack, and unearthed archival photographs for the video. Under this principal's watch, every element of the school day was focused on increasing learning. Even fun days had an instructional element. I visited one day when the school was having a fair. The children had the opportunity to throw whipped cream pies at the principal and other administrators and teachers with tickets earned previously from completing homework. The new culture celebrating the children's exponential potential became a mission pursued by students, teachers, parents, administrators, and every individual who set foot in the school. I have no doubt that the school will continue to improve. The principal set the standard and led all constituents to adopt the mission.

I have learned that the vision of the principal becomes that of the school. If the principal doesn't fully believe that the children can excel academically, or if the principal believes that the best that can be expected of poor African American children is solely a regimented environment, then that is what the school will be. It will not make academic progress. It will not produce self-disciplined, creative, problem-solving, critical thinkers. The principal—the leadership—defines what a school can become. While there are always some exceptional teachers who will produce classroom excellence wherever they may be located, to create an exceptional *school*, it takes principals who can re-envision the possibilities. They create a counter-narrative to the larger society's story of African American underachievement by writing a new and hopeful story.

The work is not easy. In this volume, some of the Black administrators and teachers are concerned about raising issues of race in their work. Their fear stems from the justifiable belief that speaking out against racially damaging policies will bring accusations of "reverse racism." For educators—teachers, principals, guidance counselors, researchers, all of us—I believe our job is to be willing to speak out against racism in education. We must be willing to reveal to the larger society policies, practices, and beliefs that support the narrative of Black inferiority. We must rewrite the story for ourselves and for our children. Educational researchers have a special responsibility. Black administrators, teachers, and students cannot speak about their experiences and have them validated in the academy or in policy circles, but if there is published research to support their views, then there is a greater chance that their views will be given some attention. And that is why it is so important to have this work documented—by the many African American and scholars of color doing such work, but especially by the White scholars, like Jeff Brooks and Gary Orfield, who are brave enough to take on the challenge. Because it *is* about race, and it's time we faced that reality squarely.

—Lisa D. Delpit

Acknowledgments

This research would not have been possible without many people's time, expertise, and effort. First and foremost, I thank the teachers and administrators of DuBois High School for sharing their insights on racism and educational leadership with me. I learned a great deal from them and hope those lessons are conveyed on these pages to a wider audience. Among scholars, Catherine A. Lugg, Fenwick W. English, Jay Paredes Scribner, Catherine Marshall, Linda Tillman, Kathleen M. Brown, Mark Gooden, Ira Bogotch, Leslie Hazle Bussey, Judy Alston, Ernestine Enomoto, Jeffrey Ayala Milligan, Joanne Marshall, Lisa A. W. Kensler, Grahaeme Hesp, Harry F. Wolcott, Mark T. Miles, Diane Hodgins, and Jackie Blount have all provided generous support in their own way. My work on this book coincided with the beginning of my association with a special group of additional scholars also doing work on race and educational leadership: Sonya Douglass Horsford, George Theoharis, Floyd Beachum, Madeline Hafner, Bradley Carpenter, Sarah Diem, Terah Venzant Chambers, Noelle Witherspoon Arnold, Carlos McCray, Elizabeth Ramalho Murakami, and Molly Killingsworth. I'm excited that this list continues to grow! I am also enthusiastic about the prospect of learning from each of them and deepening our work together over the coming years. I am especially grateful for the friendship and work of two friends and leading scholars in education, Lisa Delpit, who wrote the Foreword to this book and Bill Ayers, who consented to the interview that appears at the end. They have both been a source of inspiration and critical feedback for me. Among academic friends, a special note of thanks goes to Anthony H. Normore, Gaetane Jean-Marie, and Autumn K. Tooms for sharing their time, head, heart, and hands with me these many years. I am honored to have the three of them in my life as friends and colleagues—keep doing the right things for the right reasons! Of course there are many more friends and scholars I've neglected to mention, but who also have enriched my scholarship with their work and friendship—thanks to all of them for their contributions to our shared academic community.

Some of the work in this book was presented previously at conferences sponsored by the University Council for Educational Administration

(UCEA), the American Educational Research Association (AERA), and the Minority Student Achievement Network (MSAN), and I thank these organizations for providing a forum in which researchers can develop and safely present nascent and controversial research. In particular, I thank the AERA Leadership for Social Justice Special Interest Group and AERA Division A: Administration, Organizations, and Leadership. I also acknowledge the contributions of my colleagues and students at Florida State University, Auburn University, the University of Missouri–Columbia, and Iowa State University for their support.

I thank Jean Ward of Teachers College Press for her patience, guidance, and faith in this project. I also appreciate Emerald Publishing Group Limited, Rowman & Littlefield Publishing Group, the *Journal of School Leadership*, and the *UCEA Review* for their permission to reprint some previously published material.

A huge and heartfelt thanks also goes to my parents, Anne and Brian Brooks, and to Rick and Carol Raleigh for steadfast support.

DEDICATION

My family sacrificed more than I asked, and more than I can repay, so that this research could be completed. To my three amazing and talented daughters, Holland, Bronwyn, and Clodagh—I love you very much. Always pursue your dreams and stand up for what's right, no matter how hard that may be. It *will* be hard because you will learn in front of the world, but it *will* be worth it. To Jürgen, the newest addition to our family, we have so much yet to explore! I can't wait to be your guide and learn from you. Finally, and most important, this book is dedicated to Melanie Brooks. You are the love of my life and my best friend. You are my greatest inspiration, my confidante, my strength, my life, my soul.

Black School
White School

RACISM AND
EDUCATIONAL
(MIS)LEADERSHIP

Introduction

Racism is alive and well in the United States. That sad fact is playing out in the nation's public schools. Racism compromises the quality of instruction students receive (Collins, 2009; Delpit, 1995). Racism motivates many schools to adopt a culturally irrelevant curriculum to support that instruction (Ladson-Billings, 1992, 1995a, 1995b, 1995c, 1997). Racism undermines the fairness of assessments used to measure student academic achievement (Darling-Hammond, 1995). Racism erodes the quality of the formal and informal relationships students develop with peers and with the adult educators in their lives (Ogbu, 1978; Perry, Steele, & Hilliard, 2003). Racism is a potentially quantifiable phenomenon, measured through longstanding achievement gaps, gaps in disciplinary referrals, school (re)segregation, and a disproportionate number of students of color placed in special/remedial/lower-tracked education. Racism is also a qualitative phenomenon—studied throughout the world as a violent and oppressive sociological, anthropological, political, economic, and educational phenomenon (Fordham, 1996; Hacker, 2003; West, 1998). Of course, even calling racism a "phenomenon" is generous in that it makes abstract something all too concrete in the lives of too many Americans—at its core, racism is one person or a group's expression of contempt, of hatred, of evil, of oppression toward another person or group of people—it's important not to lose sight of that by overintellectualizing the concept.

Teachers and educational administrators are among the nation's best and brightest public intellectuals (Dantley & Tillman, 2006), but many of these people are also uncritical of deep-seated overt and covert racist values that shape who they are and how they teach or lead (Young & Laible, 2000).

Racism also undermines the quality of the professional and interpersonal relationships among these educators (Brooks & Jean-Marie, 2007), so it seems reasonable to suggest that the influence of racism on education is both direct and indirect. Racism comes through implicit and explicit institutions, it comes from people, from the home, from school, and from society, and most of us are part of its pervasive force by commission or omission (Brooks, 2007). Moreover, it means one thing to me and another

1

to you; what I may think is anti-racist, you may view as the opposite. Racism is co-constructed by the oppressor and the oppressed, among oppressors and among the oppressed; and these relationships are mediated by a great many variables and factors that are constantly changing. So, in a way, no matter how hard we try, how thoughtful we may be, we are likely part of *both* the problem *and* the solution at the same time. Does it make you upset to think that you are part of the problem? Good. It makes me angry to think that I am part of the problem, too, but I accept it as part of my efforts to unlearn the racism I have been taught by society and school.

I am White. In fact, I am a White man born into much privilege. I am the son of a celebrated college professor. I grew up largely uncritical of the privilege my skin color and social class afforded me. Over the course of the past decade I have worked hard to unlearn my miseducation about race and racism in the United States (Brooks & Tooms, 2008). That possibly unrealistic goal continues to elude me, but I have evolved in both my thinking and actions related to race and racism, and in this book I will share with you part of this ongoing journey toward increased awareness of issues and understanding of my agency to change them.

Still, while it is important to tell you something about who I am at the onset of the book, and while it does document some steps in my own development, the book is not about me. I include and comment on how this study helped me grow for two reasons. First, in qualitative research it is important to be clear about one's relationship to the topic and to the participants (Bogdan & Biklen, 1998; Scheurich, 2002). Second, I have read dozens of books and articles that suggest people need to be critical of themselves, as both researchers and people, without modeling what this looks like. In divulging my own misgivings and lack of confidence, and the evolution of my thinking about racism and educational leadership as a researcher, I invite other educational researchers, teachers, and administrators to work on unlearning their miseducation about race and racism. It will be uncomfortable at times, and it's a process more than a destination, but one well worth the struggle—for me, for you, for the schools, and for the kids.

This book, *Black School White School: Racism and Educational (Mis)Leadership*, is about how racism influenced leadership practice, and ultimately the education of students, in an urban high school. The title alludes to a central finding of the book: that while educators, students, and the community worked in the same building, the school and community in which they all lived were sharply divided along racial lines. The book begins with a single chapter that provides some basic data about race and educational leadership in the United States. The rest of the text is divided into three parts.

Part I, *From Social Justice to Racism*, documents my initial attempts to make sense of what was going on at the school. Beware! The two chapters in this part are quite technical, as they originally appeared in highly competitive peer-reviewed journals. I made an effort to transform these into a slightly "softer" read, but I also think it is important to keep them largely intact so readers get a sense of my initial understanding of the school. Chapter 2, "Distributed Leadership for Social Justice," was published originally as an article in the *Journal of School Leadership*. I enlisted my colleagues Gaetane Jean-Marie, Anthony H. Normore, and Diane W. Hodgins to help me analyze and interpret data I gathered. We combined ideas from two contemporary bodies of literature, leadership for social justice and distributed leadership, to develop a conceptual framework that explored issues of equity in the school. In my opinion, the article represents some careful and thorough work, but it also left me with the feeling that these widely used approaches to understanding leadership and equity, at least the way we used them, were lacking. I worried that by studying the fairly abstract concept of "social justice," we actually were taking the focus away from the key issue, which I was increasingly convinced had to do more specifically with racism.

Chapter 3, which Gaetane and I wrote together, originally appeared in the *Journal of Educational Administration* and looked more closely at issues of race and culture. We used an anthropological theoretical framework called a moiety that helps researchers understand the ways subcultures relate to one another. This was a cautious step forward, but an exciting one to me, as we were able to look more closely at the ways cultural anthropologists have approached the study of race and racism. I found the literature in cultural anthropology to be much more rich than anything I had read in educational administration research, where studies of race are few and far between. Considered together, these two chapters show a researcher, with the help of some astute friends and colleagues, moving from social justice to racism as a way of understanding inequity in a situated context. I am grateful to these colleagues for pushing my thinking about these issues. Working with them helped me appreciate the value of collaborating with critical friends, and engaging their ideas, questions, and perspectives encouraged me to study what was happening in the school more squarely as racism.

Part II, *Racism and Educational Misleadership*, explores issues I wasn't ready to investigate in Part I. These chapters include many passages that were as difficult to type as they were to hear when my participants said them. I present findings based on 2 years of noting observations, conducting interviews, and gathering documents. You will find both qualitative and quantitative data in these chapters. As the primary focus of the study was how race and race relations influenced the educational practice of the teachers and administrators, most data were collected from and about these professionals, yet there are also data gleaned from interactions with other stakeholders.

The third and final Part, *Lessons Learned and Possibilities for the Future*, includes Chapter 9, which summarizes key points of the study and also considers what we might take away from the study to inform subsequent research and practice. My previous book (Brooks, 2006a) focused primarily on refining theory and didn't communicate with the audience I felt mattered most—educators working in schools—by exploring and explaining the practical implications of the work and beginning a dialogue about what might be done to improve practice. While I'm proud of that book, I feel the concluding chapter was unnecessarily dense and written in a stilted, academic tone. For this reason, literature is threaded throughout this book rather than nested all in a single chapter. Part III also includes a conversation with educational scholar Bill Ayers about some of the key themes of this study and about considering them in a larger context of education and society. A brief methodological appendix concludes the book.

While this overview has provided a peek into the contents of this book, it is also necessary at the onset to make a quick comment about the manner in which data are presented. The first three chapters are fairly technical in style, being a presentation of data and two being reprinted journal articles. Part II, however, has a decidedly different, more conversational/narrative style.

CHAPTER 1

Racism and Educational (Mis)Leadership in the United States

The purpose of this chapter is to explore some concepts, trends, and projections in education regarding race and educational leadership. Toward this end, I will present information on two aspects of race—phenotype and cultural oppression—paying special attention to the multiple contexts in which these phenomena are manifest in U.S. society. As Fluehr-Lobban (2006) noted:

> Race is now viewed as a social construction that is primarily recognized by physical appearance, or phenotype. In the United States this means that Americans are socialized first to identify a person's race by skin color, and second by hair form, by facial features such as shape of the nose and lips, and eye form, along with other physical features like height. (p. 1)

Race as phenotype has to do with being defined as something by others, based solely on the way that a person looks. In U.S. schools, phenotype drives many of the ostensibly equity-related policy conversations and laws. It also has to do with the sorting and counting of students based on the way they look and via self-identification, rather than based on their academic performance. Phenotype is at the heart of racial quotas and many diversity initiatives. Looking at race this way is important in that it allows a way for us to understand marginalization, access, and opportunity at a systemic level, and in the hands of astute and ethical educational leaders such information can be key to leveraging resources toward greater systemic equity. However, looking at race as phenotype is only part of the story.

It is also important to know that "the idea of race is a human creation" (Hacker, 2003, p. 5). As a human creation, race is

> a culturally constructed phenomenon used for the purpose of domination and oppression. We understand that race is a multi-layered phenomenon that has cultural meaning at international, national and societal levels. Moreover, race

has particular meaning in individual communities, among groups, in each community, and in situ at the school site. (Brooks & Jean-Marie, 2007, p. 757)

Conceived in this manner, race is used as racism—a tool of oppression that one group (or individual) uses to dominate the other, culturally, economically, politically, and socially. In schools, many researchers have documented the consequences of racist educational practices. They have found an abundance of hidden racist curricula that advantage a White, middle-class perspective and name all others as inferior (Delpit, 1995); racist instructional pedagogy (Ladson-Billings, 1997); achievement gaps borne of culturally insensitive assessment practices (Darling-Hammond, 1995); inequitable graduation rates and instances of dropout (National Center for Education Statistics, 2007; Pearson & Newcomb, 2000); and many other informal dynamics (Tatum, 1999, 2007), some of which will be explored further in later chapters. However, before we listen to the teachers and administrators of DuBois High School to understand how these concepts play out in their day-to-day work as educators and leaders, it is important to understand the larger societal context in which they work.

RACE IN THE UNITED STATES

The United States is increasingly diverse.

> According to the U.S. Census Bureau (2004) projections for the year 2050, the non-Hispanic, White population of the United States is likely to increase by 7%. This modest increase is in stark contrast to projected increases among people of Hispanic origin (projected to increase by 188%), the Asian population (projected to increase by 213%), and the Black population (projected to increase by 71%). The same study also projects that by 2050, the non-Hispanic, White population will comprise only 50.1% of the country's total population, a sharp decline from the 77.1% of the population who reported their race as White in the 2000 census (U.S. Census Bureau, 2001). (Young & Brooks, 2008, pp. 1–2)

These projections are even more profound when connected to data from previous census reports. Examining census data from 1970 and 2000, and then comparing these with recent projections from the U.S. Census Bureau, reveals several interesting trends (see Table 1.1).

These trends and projections suggest a phenotypic shift in the composition of the country and underscore the tremendous rate at which the "'look'" of U.S. society is changing. However, as with many such analyses,

Table 1.1. Demographic Trends and Projections in the United States, 1970–2050

	1970	2000	2050
White	83.3	69.1	50.1
Black	10.9	12.3	14.6
Hispanic	4.5	12.5	24.4
Asian	1.1	3.6	8.0
Other	0.2	2.5	2.9

Sources: 1970: Hacker, 2003, p. 21; *2000:* U.S. Census Bureau, 2001; *2050:* see Young & Brooks, 2008.

there are corollary trends such as geographic distribution that also bear greater scrutiny.

While the United States is an increasingly diverse country, this diversity is not spread evenly within its borders. Indeed, while the highest percentage of White people is spread throughout the Midwest and Great Plains states, and the northern areas of the country (Figure 1.1), this is not the case for Black Americans, who are geographically concentrated in the southeastern United States, California, major metropolitan areas, and the eastern seaboard up to Massachusetts (Figure 1.2).

It stands to reason, then, that there are unique regional issues that affect the context of a study of race in general and on Black and White interactions in particular. While I am unable to divulge the exact location of the study because I don't want to compromise the confidentiality of any participants, I will say that this study occurred in the southeastern part of the country. I will provide additional information about the community later in this chapter.

RACE AND EDUCATION IN THE UNITED STATES

Given the trends discussed in the previous section, it is now important to start looking more directly at the demographics of public schools. In the 2007–2008 school year, White students constituted 59% of all students, while Black students represented 15% of the entire student population (Figure 1.3). Black students, being one of the larger minority groups in the population, have, as a group, a very different educational experience from that of their White peers (Delpit, 1995).

There are quite detailed and powerful reports that closely examine the consequences of racism in education for students, in terms of various

Figure 1.1. Regional Distribution of Percentage of White Population in the United States, 2000

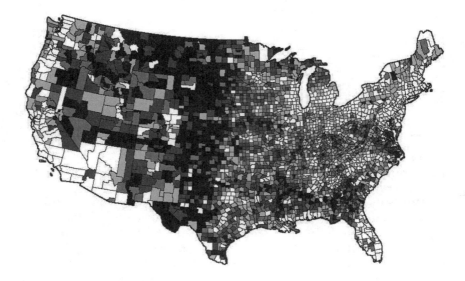

Figure 1.2. Regional Distribution by Percentage of Black Population in United States, 2000

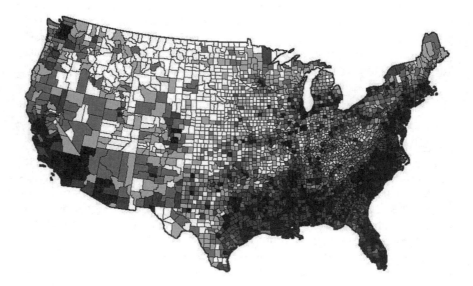

Figure 1.3. Percentage Distribution of Students by Race/Ethnicity for All U.S. Public Schools, 2007–2008

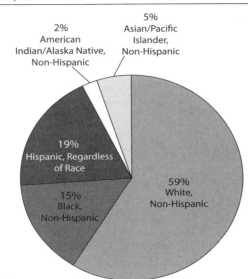

outcomes. For example, a 2004 NCES report shows a gap in terms of many educational outcomes: reading and mathematics achievement, advanced course-taking in high school, performance on Advanced Placement examinations, and performance on college entrance examinations. Moreover, the report provides powerful evidence that this is not only an achievement gap, but an education and opportunity gap as well. Take note of some of these findings:

1. Black students are twice as likely as White students to be retained, suspended, or expelled.
2. Black children have a much higher dropout rate than White students.
3. Black children are nearly half as likely as White students to use a computer at home.
4. Black girls have a much greater chance of being a teen mother than White girls.
5. Black students are twice as likely as White students to not have finished high school.

In addition to a disparity in the numbers of White and Black students, the racial breakdown of the teaching population likewise is profoundly dominated by the majority race (Figure 1.4). The numbers shrink even further when we scrutinize the percentages of Black and White principals in U.S. public schools (Figure 1.5). Interestingly, the number of Black school principals increases dramatically when we enter the core urban centers of the country (Figure 1.6), schools that also feature the highest concentrations of students of color.

Public schools in the United States, then, show several trends related to the phenotypic composition of the student, teacher, and administrator populations. First, the population of the country and of the schools will grow increasingly diverse over the coming decades. Second, there is some evidence that this diversity will be increasingly widespread and not confined to large urban centers. Third, there is a racial funnel effect in the public schools. That is, the Black student population is quite small at 15%, but the percentage of Black teachers is even lower at 8%. At first glance it seems positive that nationally 11% of principals are Black, but these are concentrated primarily in public schools in the nation's urban centers, which traditionally have the highest administrator turnover rate and face the most significant educational problems (Strizek, Pittsonberger, Riordan, Lyter, & Orlofsky, 2006). Moreover, this means that there is a great possibility that Black students will not have a Black teacher, and

Figure 1.4. Percentage Distribution of Teachers by Race/Ethnicity for all U.S. Public Schools, 2007–2008

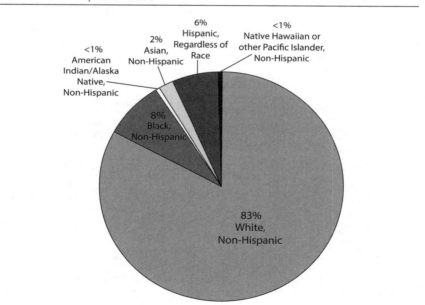

Figure 1.5. Percentage Distribution of All School Principals by Race/Ethnicity, 2003–2004

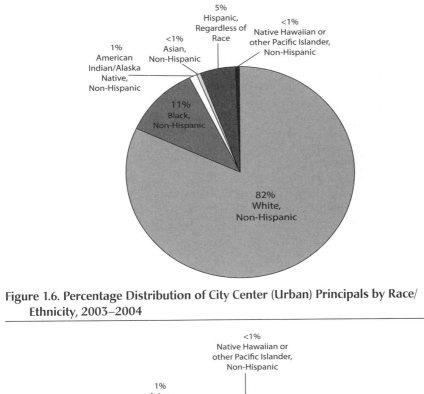

Figure 1.6. Percentage Distribution of City Center (Urban) Principals by Race/Ethnicity, 2003–2004

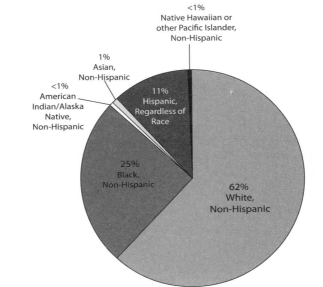

that Black teachers will not work for a Black principal. Fourth, while there are few Black public school principals, these principals generally practice leadership in the most challenging schools, making their tenures shorter and the work more difficult.

MULHOLLAND FALLS AND DuBOIS HIGH SCHOOL: A CONTEXT TO STUDY RACISM AND EDUCATIONAL LEADERSHIP

Mulholland Falls, the pseudonymous city where this study took place, is in the southeastern United States. There were approximately 250,000 people in the city limits. The racial makeup of the city at the time of the study was approximately 57% White, 38% African American, 1% Native American, 2% Asian, 1% Pacific Islander, and 1% other races. Hispanics or Latinos of any race were approximately 6% of the population and non-Hispanic Whites were 55% of the population.

The city saw tremendous growth over the past 30 years, and, indeed, archival data show that the population nearly doubled during that time. Not coincidentally, this growth accompanied the swelling enrollment of the city's two large state universities, one that had transformed itself from a women-only teaching college into a Carnegie-classified, research-intensive institution, and the other a historically Black university that had developed and maintained an excellent academic reputation for nearly a century. "They are good schools," many DuBois High School educators explained. In fact, most educators at DuBois were trained at one of these two schools. Many proudly proclaimed their allegiance whenever the opportunity allowed, and they displayed banners in their classrooms and offices that announced their affiliation. However, educators explained that although scholastic membership was one of the most overt dynamics that affected the city's social and cultural norms, it was only one manifestation of a more pervasive culture of division. As one teacher intimated, "We hang the banners and joke about it, but when you get right down to it, the cultural differences are much greater."

According to educators at DuBois High School, the city is sharply segregated along racial lines, with a distinction drawn between the so-called Black and White cultures. Educators explained that social interaction in the community is almost exclusively race-specific. As one assistant principal suggested, "It's really two completely different towns-within-a-town—very little interaction." Black and White educators alike could easily list Black and White neighborhoods, schools, restaurants, cultural events, holidays, prominent community members, and institutions. One White administrator noted, "That's the way it's always been here. The

Black folks do their thing, and the White folks do something else. We go to different football games on Saturdays, and we eat at different restaurants. Of course, we mix to some degree, but I think that the sense of racial separation is much stronger than the sense of solidarity. It's a divided community, and it has been for a long time." Regardless of which group they claimed to be members of, educators were conscious of the way that race, more than any other characteristic, defined the social and cultural norms of the community's people.

Educators described DuBois High School as one of the "Black schools" in town. At the time of the study, the district employed 80 teachers at the school, a principal, three assistant principals, an academic dean, and a dozen educational specialists to serve approximately 1,300 children, grades 9–12. The educational staff was split almost into halves, phenotypically speaking: 37 White, 39 Black. One teacher identified herself as Hispanic, and another teacher self-identified as Arab.

According to educators, DuBois is a school with significant challenges exacerbated by racial dynamics. It serves a poverty-stricken area of the city, and students have fared poorly on standardized examinations for several years. Many of DuBois' students read at an elementary school level and drop out of school before they finish. However, many others stay in despite low achievement. It is common among the school's general education population that a student might be 18 years old and in 9th grade or as old as 22 if diagnosed with a learning disability. As educators explained, "A significant number of students have a bleak academic future," and as another long-serving teacher lamented, "Many students end up in low-wage service jobs, into lives of crime, or in the welfare system." That being said, students and neighborhood families have a sense of pride, and they value the school's academic and athletic traditions, both of which are significant. Over the course of its history, the school has won state championships in nearly every sport, although the banners that hang from the rafters of the gymnasium are now quite faded; the glory years seem long ago.

Academically, DuBois High School is a paradox. Whereas the general education population is low-performing, the school houses an International Baccalaureate (IB) program that sends students to elite universities on full academic scholarships every year. At DuBois, the IB program is essentially a school within a school. The program has its own operating budget, and teachers in the program answer directly to the IB program coordinator rather than the school's administrators. Additionally, IB teachers have their own lounge, which is the only operational lounge in the school. Furthermore, IB teachers receive a stipend every time their students pass an IB examination, which can amount to several thousand dollars of extra money for teachers in the program. As a social phenomenon, the IB program is both a uniting and a dividing force.

Like the country, region, state, and community, DuBois High School is divided along racial lines. Of course, these lines are constantly moving and have been evolving for quite a while as people and ideas flow into and out of the community and school. The subsequent chapters represent my initial attempts to understand how racism influenced education in the school, beginning with the concepts of social justice and distributed leadership.

Part I

FROM SOCIAL JUSTICE TO RACISM

CHAPTER 2

Distributed Leadership for Social Justice

Over the past 2 decades, educational leadership scholars have made significant contributions to our understanding of the ways educators can, and do, lead for social justice in schools (Marshall & Gerstl-Pepin, 2005; Marshall & Oliva, 2006). Conceptual research suggests that a social justice orientation toward educational leadership practice and research promises to lead to a greater understanding of "how institutionalized theories, norms, and practices in schools and society lead to social, economic, and educational inequities" (Dantley & Tillman, 2006, p. 17). Social justice scholars argue that leadership practice informed by such understanding will empower and enable leaders to better serve traditionally marginalized students and dismantle longstanding norms that privilege certain students at the expense of others. Empirical studies in this line of inquiry support the contention that school leadership can positively influence these dynamics, but that such work is fraught with organizational barriers that perpetuate inequity within schools (e.g., Gooden, 2005) and with deeply rooted social-psychological dynamics that permeate all levels of society (Scheurich & Young, 1997).

While many educators throughout school systems can find inspiration in the call to ameliorate hegemony and work toward more ethical and equitable educational practice, school leaders are uniquely positioned to facilitate meaningful and substantive change at the building level. It is therefore incumbent on educational leadership researchers to explore social justice *in situ*, and to develop, test, and refine theories that might provide a foundation for subsequent social justice research and ultimately more equitable practices in schools (Bogotch et al., 2008; Brooks, 2008). In response to this imperative, this research explored key social justice concepts at the building level by using a conceptual framework grounded in two heretofore discrete lines of theory: social justice and distributed leadership (Spillane, 2006).

Viewing leadership practice from a distributed perspective suggests that specific contextual factors, situational factors, individuals, and artifacts influence one another to create a protean phenomenon termed "leadership practice" (Spillane, 2006). Importantly, when conceived in this manner, leadership practice is "stretched over" all members of an organization rather than being a particular set of roles or behaviors enacted by a formal administrator in a specific and rational decision-making process. Instead, leadership practice is a fluid phenomenon that changes from situation to situation, from context to context, and that evolves over time. Although distributed leadership has been fairly criticized for failing to take into account certain sociopolitical dynamics of organizations (Maxcy & Nguyen, 2006), and can be criticized as a "difference-blind" theory (Larson & Murtadha, 2002), the ambiguity of the distributed leadership theory is actually a *strength* in that it allows researchers a useful framework for identifying certain patterns of leadership practice. While not explicitly stated as such, several studies have adopted this approach (e.g., Goldstein, 2004; Spillane, 2005). In coupling the distributed leadership theory with certain social justice concepts, the intent is to make both a conceptual and an empirical contribution to each of these important areas of inquiry and to explore the ways they might intertwine and/or be mutually exclusive. Accordingly, the twofold purpose of this chapter is to explore the manner in which social justice leadership practice is distributed throughout a particular school setting, and also to investigate the efficacy of an exploratory conceptual framework, distributed leadership for social justice.

SCHOOL LEADERSHIP: A DISTRIBUTED PERSPECTIVE

While the term *distributed leadership* is used broadly in educational research literature, for the purposes of this book, "distributed leadership" denotes a particular theoretical perspective on leadership practice (Spillane, 2006; Spillane, Halverson, & Diamond, 2004). Importantly, distributed leadership should not be confused or conflated with other seemingly similar strains of educational research such as shared governance, democratic leadership, teacher leadership, team leadership, delegation, collective decision making, and so on. Grounded in sociological and psychological inquiry, distributed leadership has evolved into a perspective for analyzing leadership practice that deviates from many traditions of educational leadership inquiry in that it does not prescribe as leadership any specific traits, characteristics, dispositions, attitudes, organizational positions, roles, or behaviors. Instead, when viewed from a distributed perspective, leadership practice is an organizational phenomenon enacted differently at each site and in each situation by both formal and informal leaders who interact with and influence an ever-changing set of artifacts and tools (Pounder, Ogawa, & Adams, 1995; Spillane, 2005).

From a distributed perspective, leadership practice occurs as three discrete organizational components interact over time: situation, leaders, and followers (see Figure 2.1).

For the purposes of this work, *situation* refers to the particular routines and tools that constrain and enable leadership practice (Spillane, 2006). Routines of various types are common in schools and include everything from seemingly mundane tasks like walking through a particular section of the school on the way to one's classroom or office to the regular schedule of multiyear strategic plans. Routines, then, are patterns of leadership that may include dynamics such as social norms, incentives, sanctions, interpersonal dynamics, and internal and external communications. As Spillane (2006) explains:

> Tools are externalized representations of ideas that are used by people in their practice. Tools include assessment data, observation protocols for evaluating teachers, lesson plans, and student academic work. These tools mediate how people practice, shaping interactions among leaders and followers in particular ways. (p. 18)

Figure 2.1. A Conceptual Model of Distributed Leadership

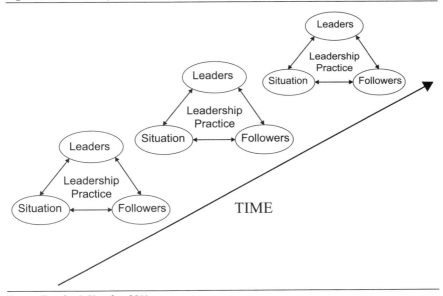

Source: Brooks & Kensler, 2011

In this work, the terms *leaders* and *followers* are used in particular ways. When we discuss leaders we are speaking of multiple formal and informal leaders, who may or may not occupy particular positions in the organization. Leadership often is enacted collaboratively as two or more leaders practice in a particular context and situation (Spillane, 2006). Importantly, leaders may practice differently, and these variations also may differ from situation to situation, from context to context, and over time. In a sense, leadership occurs as a phenomenon between multiple leaders, each of whom contributes to the practice in a unique manner. Leaders are distinguished from followers in that followers engage in routines influenced and/or established by leaders. It is important to note that leadership is not something done to followers; followers instead make an equal contribution to leadership practice and have a reciprocal influence on the routines, tools, and leaders with whom they interact to create leadership activity (Spillane, 2006). Again, when viewed from a distributed perspective, people in formal positions of authority, such as a principal, dean, or department chair, may be followers in a given situation or may assume certain roles in particular situations. School leadership practice, then, occurs as these contextual factors interact in an organizational context and influence the articulation and attainment of goals, and the orientation toward and completion of tasks. Among important topics this research has addressed are the way leadership is distributed among teachers during comprehensive school reform implementation in elementary schools (Camburn, Rowan, & Taylor, 2003), the enactment of accountability policy (Spillane, Diamond, Burch, Hallett, Jita, & Zoltners, 2002), how teachers reconstruct their practice based on external reform demands (Spillane, 1999), and how leadership is enacted at the departmental and classroom levels differentially depending on the subject of instruction.

The distributed leadership theory has been used to explore and explain various aspects of school leadership, but it has earned both admirers and detractors. Distributed leadership has been alternately lauded as a significant theoretical advance that improves our conceptual understanding of leadership practice and derided as yet another "difference-blind" model that fails to account for the political and power dimensions of equity issues such as race, sexism, and class bias (Larson & Murtadha, 2002; Maxcy & Nguyen, 2006). While it has these limitations, the absence of these components in the model creates a useful ambiguity that allows researchers to explore the distribution of many forms of leadership practice. Put differently, while there is nothing in the model to guide researchers toward a greater sensitivity of political, power, and equity dimensions in leadership practice, there is likewise nothing *preventing* scholars from exploring these issues from a distributed perspective. Spillane's model may not purposively and explicitly include such dynamics in the model described above, but we can ameliorate this "shortcoming" by using the distributed leadership theory as a conceptual foundation and supplementing it with additional theoretical constructs. This research combines inquiry on leadership for social justice with the distributed leadership theory to help frame an investigation of how leadership for social justice is stretched over formal and informal leaders throughout an organization. Given this orientation, it is important to explain how leadership for social justice is conceived in this study.

LEADERSHIP FOR SOCIAL JUSTICE: FROM ABSTRACT IDEALS TO EVERYDAY PRACTICE

Scholars in many fields of inquiry study social justice (Cohen, 1986; Marshall & Oliva, 2006). Multi- and interdisciplinary strains of social justice inquiry include, at their core, concepts and issues such as equity, equality, liberation, emancipation, racism, sexism, discrimination, and oppression (English, 2005). Research on leadership for social justice in educational leadership has been conducted from various critical theoretical perspectives.

Social justice leadership seeks whole-school reform that bases teaching and learning on students' creation of knowledge that will liberate them from the ways in which they

> have already been classified and identified by dominant discourses. This means discovering new ways of understanding [themselves] and one another, refusing to accept the dominant culture's characterizations of [their] practices and desires, and re-defining them from within resistant cultures. (Sawicki, 1991, p. 44)

Through problem-posing and -solving, students learn to question which knowledge is valued and why; they examine their access to opportunities for intellectual, economic, and social advancement; and they learn to reach an understanding of knowing that they know (Freire, 1989; Sernak, 2006). The subsequent sections focus on a few core ideas related to leadership for social justice, and then show how they looked in the school.

LEADERS AS TRANSFORMATIONAL PUBLIC INTELLECTUALS

Freire (1989) contends that all human beings, regardless of social and economic function, perform as intellectuals by constantly interpreting and giving meaning to the world and by participating in a particular conception of the world. Moreover, the oppressed need to develop their own organic and transformative intellectuals who can learn with such groups while simultaneously helping to foster modes of self-education and struggle against various forms of oppression (Giroux, 1988). It is critical to view school leaders as intellectuals if we are to rethink and reform the traditions and conditions that have prevented them from assuming their full potential as active, reflective scholars and practitioners.

Giroux (1988) suggests a need to rethink and restructure the nature of school leadership. School leaders who become transformative intellectuals provide "the moral, political and pedagogical leadership for those who engage in the transformative critique of the conditions of oppression" (p. 152). In other words, we must provide a theoretical basis for examining leadership work as a form of intellectual labor, rather than defining it in purely instrumental or technical terms. He further asserts the necessity to make the political more pedagogical by using forms of pedagogy that treat students as critical agents, make knowledge problematic, and utilize critical and affirming dialogue. Transformative intellectuals take seriously the need to give students an active voice in their learning experiences and to connect their culture to classroom practice.

LEADERSHIP FOR BRIDGING AND CONNECTING PEOPLE

Bridge people (Merchant & Shoho, 2006) seek to connect ideas, individuals, and institutions not commonly in collaboration in educational contexts—they cross boundaries and borders for the good of students. Part of their agenda for social justice is to decrease the achievement gap, increase the quality of schools for all students, and provide necessary resources. Many school leaders espouse a belief in and articulate a commitment to social justice, but there is a tendency to separate social justice from daily practices that have a direct impact on the "haves and have nots." Bridge people as social justice school leaders embody certain characteristics that enable them to view social justice as integral to practices (Marshall & Young, 2006) that impact educational objectives (i.e., increased student achievement). In a study of eight individuals who were recognized as leaders for social justice and equity, Merchant and Shoho (2006) found that these individuals shared a number of characteristics. To a name a few, they included a (1) strong orientation toward social justice and equity issues instilled in their early years; (2) strong sense of purpose and belief to overcome obstacles; (3) powerful experiences of marginalization that shaped their determination to fight against injustices for all; and (4) an awareness of the influence of the social/ political movements of the 1950s and 1960s.

SCHOOL LEADERS AS CRITICAL ACTIVISTS

In order to understand, promote, and enact social justice, school leaders first must develop a heightened and critical awareness of oppression, exclusion, and marginalization. To return to Freire (1989), critical consciousness, or *conscientizacão*, "refers to learning to perceive social, political, and economic contradictions, and to take action against the oppressive elements of reality" (p. 58). Freire's *conscientizacātion* is "the possession of critical consciousness, that is, understanding and addressing the reality one lives and, simultaneously, one's consciousness of that reality" (Lankshear, 1993, as cited in Sernak, 2006). Fundamental to attaining critical consciousness is dialogue, for it opens the spaces for free, creative exploration of complex and subtle issues (Senge, 1990), thus requiring critical thinking.

A social justice "orientation is taught overtly in some preservice educational leadership programs learned on the job or in professional development by other leaders, and likely never learned by others" (Brooks & Miles, 2006). Children who live in poverty and/or who are minorities racially or ethnically need more than a "banking" education (Freire, 1989). They need to learn for liberation and freedom, that is, they need to question the answers, not answer the questions, in order to take control of their own lives (Sernak, 2006). Without a leader's willingness to deal with dialogue, assumptions, and biases, differences continue to be ignored. The power structure, hegemonic and hierarchical, continues as is; schools, despite the rhetoric of vision, researched pedagogy, and community-shared and -supported educational goals, remain the same. Freire (1989) advocated that education for poor children should be about human and community development, about understanding who the children are, personally, culturally, and socially. It is about becoming visible to self and others. The poet David Whyte (2001) eloquently illustrates this sentiment: "To be human is to become visible while carrying what is hidden as a gift to others" (p. 190).

However, as Brooks and Miles (2006) note:

> Awareness of social injustices is not sufficient, school leaders must act when they identify inequity. School leaders are not only uniquely positioned to influence equitable educational practice, their proactive involvement is imperative. (p. 107)

Leaders who are critical activists take this call to heart; these are educational leaders who move from awareness to intent, and then ultimately to action.

It is important to note that the work of critical activists can be both difficult and dangerous. Speaking or acting against entrenched formal and informal social structures, norms, and processes can lead to interpersonal and institutional reprisals. Further, critical activists face potential threats both from inside their organizations and from external stakeholders if they challenge longstanding traditions, regardless of whether they do so from a moral high ground (Larson & Murtadha, 2002). Given these ideas, which individually and collectively frame our thinking about the subject, the following sections of this chapter focus on how leadership for social justice was distributed throughout DuBois High School.

TRANSFORMATIONAL PUBLIC INTELLECTUALISM, STRETCHED ACROSS A SCHOOL

At DuBois High, teachers, administrators, and school staff practiced transformational public intellectualism in various ways during the course of the study. While this took many forms, which are discussed in greater detail below, broadly speaking these activities were either: (a) practiced by certain leaders in multiple situations and with multiple followers, or (b) practiced by somewhat fluid subcommunities of scholars. These subcommunities were at times formal units within the organizational structure of the school, such as departments or grade-level instructional task forces designed to address particular areas of student need. At other times they were informal clusters of educators practicing spontaneous transformational public intellectualism on behalf of the students. While varying from situation to situation and over time, teacher leaders practicing transformational public intellectualism generally interacted with other teacher-followers and student-followers. Administrators rarely followed teachers' transformational public intellectual practice, except when the situation involved instructional and curricular situations in which implementation would demand classroom autonomy. In most noninstructional, nonclassroom situations, administrators exercised their formal right to act without the input of teachers; whole-school reform issues, budget issues, policy interpretation and implementation, or issues regarding enforcement of school regulations were the sole purview of the administrative team.

DISTRIBUTED ANTI-INTELLECTUALISM VERSUS LIBERATION LEADERSHIP

Analyzing leadership through the distributed perspective revealed a tension in the school that took many different forms, but remained constant throughout the duration of the study, a tension between anti-intellectual leadership and leadership for liberation. By anti-intellectual we mean that on many occasions, decisions with broad-ranging implications were made with little or no debate, input, or logical rationale. For example, during the second year of data collection for this study, the school learned that it would be housing a health education magnet program. In the early days at the school level, this meant that the administration needed to appoint a director for the program and see to it that funds allocated to the purchase of related instructional resources were used to purchase highly specialized medical instruments and apparatus, in addition to appropriate textbooks. The decision about whom to appoint as director became fraught with organizational politics. Initially, the principal announced to his administrative team that the assistant principal for curriculum would assume the director's role for the prestigious program. This decision was not popular at the district office, and a personnel director suggested that another assistant principal, one with much less experience, be made director. The principal was unhappy with this suggestion but acquiesced to this informal fiat by briefly considering the possibility of making an administrative assistant who had worked as a nurse in a previous career the director. This, too, fell through since the district ruled that the director must be a licensed teacher. In the end, a director was never named and an assistant principal with no experience in health purchased all program materials, many of which proved to be inappropriate. The following year, the principal hired a director after conducting an external search. This director, who had experience as a health teacher and seemed like an inspired hire, ultimately resigned 3 months into the school year, in part because of her perception that she did not have the proper resources to instruct students, and in part because she felt that she was being made a scapegoat for the program's shortcomings, most of which were out of her control. After the director resigned, she was never replaced, and, in fact, her students roamed the halls during her assigned instructional hours. These sorts of anti-intellectual leadership practices—that is, leadership uninformed by reason, information, or meaningful dialogue—occurred over and over throughout the study.

In contrast, the principal and assistant principals comported themselves with great leadership acumen in other situations, interacting with and acting as followers to practice liberation leadership. Moreover, observations and interviews revealed numerous occasions when teachers acted as transformational public intellectuals. These were instances when transformational public intellectualism was practiced in a manner that facilitated critical dialogue around issues and articulated a course of action, which then was pursued. For example, on many occasions, teachers, administrators, and students would act as leaders who critically analyzed

instructional and curricular issues, noted oppressive practice, and recti-
fied the situation by initiating a formal change. In particular, several teachers, administrators, and students questioned, from time to time, the nature
of the "hidden curriculum" at the school. Examples of these leadership
practices included:

1. A student-led inquiry about whether certain resources used
    to teach an upper-level philosophy course were Anglocentric
    and possibly racist. One student assumed leadership in that
    he engaged many others by articulating an informed and
    reasoned intellectual critique of the works in question. Other
    students leapt to this student's side and joined in a campaign to
    reconsider certain materials.
2. A librarian-initiated effort to weed the Media Center's books of
    inappropriate materials. Many works in the collection contained
    racial slurs and eugenics-based materials that suggested certain
    peoples were inherently inferior to others. Although this
    "weeding" of the collection threatened to put the school out of
    compliance with accreditation standards for the total number
    of books on hand, the librarian explained that she would rather
    jeopardize accreditation, as "books based on the idea that the
    'negro' has inherent moral, physical, and intellectual deficiencies
    are not acceptable, both because they are offensive and grossly
    inaccurate. I refuse to be a part of the perpetuation of such
    horrible ideas."

While observations suggested many such instances of liberation leadership, there was little evidence that these practices evolved over time.
Educators in the school seemed largely content to practice this form of
leadership on a situation-to-situation basis—these were random acts of social justice. Leaders often would use a perceived injustice as a rallying cry
and articulate a particular, tangible goal, and when it was accomplished,
the leaders and followers would discontinue their interaction.

INTERNATIONAL BACCALAUREATE PROGRAM:
ONE SUBCOMMUNITY OF SCHOLARS FOR SOCIAL JUSTICE

One particular subcommunity of scholars practiced transformational public intellectualism as a sustained operational norm. The school's International Baccalaureate (IB) program was a hotbed of debate, critical inquiry,
and instructional and curriculum innovation. There was an obvious esprit
de corps among the teachers affiliated with the IB program, and perhaps

more important, these teachers consistently engaged their students in intellectual discourse. IB classes were the only ones in the school where students and teachers engaged issues of race, class, poverty, sexual orientation, oppression, and privilege; and they did so on a regular basis. Teachers in the IB program endeavored to create a safe place for this discourse in their classrooms and among their teacher subcommunity. Teachers did this both formally and informally, by establishing discourse-facilitating rules in their classrooms and by sharing these rules and the lessons based on them with peers.

IB teacher dialogues about social justice issues clearly evolved over time. This appeared to be due to a few reasons. First, the attrition rate among IB teachers was lower than that of the school's non-IB teaching population. This allowed teachers to sustain dialogues over a period of years with one another and with students matriculating through the program. Second, the IB teachers worked hard to create spaces where intellectual dialogue could occur. For example, the IB teachers maintained and used the only operational teachers' lounge in the school. Observations of this space over a 2-year period indicated that it was a safe space for intellectual debate, sharing of ideas, and raising doubts and insecurities. As one teacher, speaking for many, explained: "I live for those lunches. They are an amazing source of ideas and inspiration. In fact, I thought about leaving DuBois a few years ago, but I stayed because of those lunches. And it's the best decision I could have made." Third, IB teachers were much more aware of both current educational events *and* the school's history than were other teachers. Many IB teachers could name the school's past four principals (whose tenure spanned a collective 20 years) and discuss their relative merits and shortcomings. Interestingly, this institutional knowledge included both veteran and neophyte teachers, and it afforded them a different, and longitudinal, perspective from that of most other teachers in the school. Moreover, the IB teachers' knowledge of up-to-the-minute policy discussions at the federal, state, and local levels meant that they were able to debate the relative merits of various initiatives and decide whether ideas "coming down the pipe" were worth instituting ahead of time. (The IB program is explored in much greater detail in Chapter 6.)

BLACK LEADERS AS TRANSFORMATIONAL PUBLIC INTELLECTUALS

Another important leadership practice related to transformational public intellectualism was enacted by the school's Black leaders. While there was variation among these leaders in terms of their perspectives on leadership, certain themes arose from interview and observational data. Black leaders consistently explained that they felt a responsibility to individual students and to the town's Black community to be intellectual role models. To one mathematics teacher, for example, this meant recruiting Black students into his advanced courses and showing them the career possibilities that can "come alive when you understand and love math." He explained, "I want to show them that a Black man can have a good life doing brain work. Many kids don't see that in the community." To other leaders this also meant adopting "professional" dress and mannerisms. While these leaders were aware that dressing a certain way was not intellectual activity per se, several believed that this outward expression showed Black youth a dimension of their culture that was underrepresented outside of school. As the principal explained: "I like for them to see that a Black man can look sharp—it implies something about having a sharp mind, too. I always tell them it's because I studied hard."

BRIDGEWORK AS DISTRIBUTED LEADERSHIP FOR SOCIAL JUSTICE

Observation and interview data showed that leaders throughout the school engaged in bridgework leadership practice. That is, they sought to connect individuals and groups to external resources intended to help them overcome various forms of inequity. This leadership practice was easy to recognize and was a form of leadership practice for social justice that many educators were proud of having facilitated. However, while in the broadest sense most educators are likely to agree with leveraging external resources toward the end of providing student services, we learned early in the study that bridgework is not without challenges and obstacles.

COMMUNICATION AND AWARENESS: CRITICAL ASPECTS OF BRIDGEWORK

Interviews revealed that while many dynamics are in play as educators seek to conduct bridgework for social justice, two key phenomena had a tremendous influence over the success of this sort of leadership practice: communication and awareness. With respect to communication, leaders and followers alike expressed frustration with both informal and formal barriers that thwarted their efforts to reach out to external organizations and people. As one teacher explained:

> The physical layout of this building is a problem. You can't trust word-of-mouth as a communication strategy. Also, not everyone here has a working computer so that is an issue within the school. Now,

when you try to communicate with parents in this community, many of them don't have access to a computer. Another thing I'd like to do is enlist the help of local Black churches, who are represented by some of the most respected leaders in the Black community, but we are all confused about what churches can and can't do in the schools.

This quote also addresses another source of frustration: The tools and routines used to communicate were appropriate for some forms of communication, but ineffective for others. Communications structures in the school worked well for some purposes, such as the way that the administrative team worked with department chairs to distribute formal instructional and policy information, but these same avenues of communication did not work for other purposes, such as communicating with parents, community members, and other external stakeholders. Although many leaders recognized the need to establish new tools and routines, none had stepped forward to lead the organization on this issue.

Awareness was a second important aspect of bridgework. This largely took two distinct forms: (1) a lack of awareness about equity issues in general, and (2) a lack of awareness about what bridges could be built between the school and the community to address issues of inequity once they had been identified. These two aspects with regard to awareness seemed connected to the issue of communication in that it may have been that the lack of dialogue among educators at the school and between these educators and external constituents was hampered by ineffective, yet institutionalized, tools and routines. It was, for example, quite striking to hear the enlightened levels of awareness with regard to bridgework and equity among teachers in the IB teacher subcommunity when contrasted to general education teachers, who for the most part did not share lunches or a stable membership in their teacher subcommunities.

BUILDING BRIDGES FOR SOCIAL JUSTICE:
INDIVIDUAL AND INSTITUTIONAL LEADERSHIP

Bridgework leadership practice at DuBois generally took one of two forms, individual and institutional. By making this distinction we are drawing attention to those whom the bridgework leadership practice was intended to benefit. That is, individual bridgework leadership took place in those instances when a leader reached out to leverage external resources in a manner intended to benefit a single student. This happened in many situations and often involved leaders interacting with extra-organizational followers. This type of leadership was illustrated by an art teacher who explained how she made a student aware of and helped him find an opportunity that allowed him to attend college, which the student would not have done but for her bridgework.

> [The student came into my class] as a senior. I was looking through his sketchbook. I said, "I love that school bus. Why don't you do a print out of it?" It took him almost a whole 6 weeks to do the print. . . . At the state art show he won an award down there. And one of the judges happened to be a representative of a college. From one school bus the kid won a $10,000 scholarship . . . he didn't even know he had that opportunity. He didn't even know anyone besides me thought he was an artist.

Other bridgework leadership for social justice was more institutional in nature, designed to address inequity for groups of students rather than individuals. These forms of leadership practice commonly took the form of community outreach programs, such as a school-to-work program that offered employment prospects to students who needed to work to develop job skills and in many instances to help support their families. These programs, and others like them, offered systemic forms of support and were designed to address inequity borne of both differential cultural capital and time pressures, as students in this program left school early to make it on time for their shift. This program had evolved over a number of years and was supported by both locally owned businesses and national corporations.

DISTRIBUTED CRITICAL ACTIVISM

Many educational leaders throughout the school explained that since they had been working at DuBois High, they had become more aware of equity issues and had developed their critical consciousness toward equity issues. That being said, while there was much promise in such assertions, it was also clear that many of these same potential leaders for social justice had difficulty making the transition from awareness to action.

DISTRIBUTED *CONSCIENTIZAÇÃO*

Teachers at DuBois commonly talked about how their critical consciousness with regard to equity issues developed through stages over time. While certainly each individual experience was somewhat idiosyncratic, there were certain issues that every interviewee explained s/he had to consider. First, educators explained that they had to first make sense of the culture of the school and the community. Educators came to DuBois with diverse personal and professional experiences, ranging from teachers who had grown up in the Cabrini-Green housing project on Chicago's north side to educators whose primary experience was in culturally homogeneous rural settings. All of these educators went through an assimilation process that prompted them to evaluate their past experiences with equity concerns within their new environment, both in school and out of school. This took educators varying amounts of time, and each admitted to making mistakes and erroneous assumptions along the way. Second, educators suggested that in addition to taking in new information and combining it with their experiences, they had to learn the informal organizational norms and policies and procedures of the school and district so that they understood the constraints on what they could and couldn't do professionally. To some educators, this was a process of trial and error wherein they did what they thought was right and found out later whether they had followed protocol. Other teachers felt compelled to learn the ins and outs of the system before acting. However, regardless of technique, once educators acquired this information and made sense of it, they then had the potential to become leaders for social justice; many did.

For example, the IB program coordinator was a civil rights activist as a teacher before she took her coordinator's position. Along with several other White women, she had led a major curriculum revision on behalf of Black students in a rural Alabama town in the late 1960s. As she described it, this was a high-profile battle fought in the spotlight of national media attention.

> We took on everyone, because everyone came out with guns blazing. The Good Old Boys were out in force; so was the KKK. We received death threats and we were constantly told to shut up and be more lady-like. To me, though, there was no higher calling, and really I still feel that way today. People like me—White people like me—have always enjoyed privilege in this country. I can use that privilege for myself or I can try to use it for others; it's my choice and one I have to make every day. I don't always get it right, but I do my best to learn from my mistakes and to find new ways to make a difference. Mostly that means recognizing issues and then intervening when something isn't being done aboveboard or with all students' best interests in mind.

Not every educator was so outspoken, nor did every teacher claim or consistently exhibit such devotion to issues of equity. However, the IB coordinator behaved in accord with this attitude on many issues, and observations showed her a tireless activist for equity, particularly on racial issues, but also with respect to sexual orientation, gender, and other issues of difference. However, it must be said that while she was one of the more outspoken and visible critical activist leaders at DuBois, there were many other forms of critical activism at the school.

SOFT REVOLUTIONS AND HARD REVOLUTIONS: ACTIVISTS TAKING A STAND IN DIFFERENT WAYS

Critical activists took one of two basic approaches to leadership practice as critical activists, initiating either soft or hard revolutions (see Postman & Weingartner, 2000). This meant that they acted either as "soft revolutionaries" who learned the informal and formal systems of the school and district and worked within these to lead for social justice or as "hard revolutionaries" who worked from outside the system to effect change. The IB coordinator quoted above is an example of a hard revolutionary. Upon identifying inequity, she usually felt that the best strategy was to confront the issue head-on, by naming it and then articulating a manner in which the inequity could be addressed. This was effective in many instances, and proved a poor tactic in others. Moreover, because of the coordinator's political capital, she felt empowered to use her outspoken tactics. Other critical activist leaders for social justice took a more subtle approach. For example, as one social studies teacher explained, he confined his activism to the classroom, and sought to instill in his students a questioning mentality, rather than be an outspoken critic of a system he saw as largely unresponsive or threatening.

> I respect what [the IB coordinator] does, and it's important. But it isn't the way I can effect change. I don't have tenure and I'm fearful that I could be fired if I said some of the things she does. I see inequity, but my way of addressing it is through a critical approach to the teaching of history. I assign students to conduct critical histories of the school, of the community, of the government, and even their families. My approach to addressing equity is more subtle, but I think it is effective. Kids walk out of here looking at the world through more critical eyes.

IS LEADERSHIP FOR SOCIAL JUSTICE ENOUGH?

Knowledge and understanding about the link between social justice theory and distributed leadership models and practices can benefit aspiring and practicing school leaders. Theory and practice, advocacy and action to counter injustice have emerged from civil rights, feminist, postmodern, critical, multicultural, and other movements. Researchers indicate that grounded in these movements, social justice leaders strive for critique rather than conformity, compassion rather than competition, democracy rather than bureaucracy, polyphony rather than silencing, inclusion rather than exclusion, liberation rather than domination, and action for change rather than inaction that preserves inequity (e.g., Brooks, 2006b; Evans, Axelrod, & Langberg, 2004; Furman, 2004; Lambert et al., 1995; Larson & Murtadha, 2002; Lee & McKerrow, 2005).

Among the common definitions of equity are access, proportional outcomes, equality, political change, and social and institutional change. In support of Jean-Marie (2006) and Lambert and colleagues (1995), equitable practices and behaviors from school leaders are needed "that transform systems that promote inclusively-oriented educational environments" (p. 6). Quick and Normore (2004) assert that true leaders understand that their "actions speak louder than words," and that they must "practice what they preach" for inevitably they "shall reap what they sow" (p. 345). Although these adages are cliché, they serve as a map for the educational leader because of the powerful evidence of experience.

Educational leaders in this study testified that the culture, climate, and community that they influence in turn influence their leadership. Similar to prior studies (e.g., Donaldson, 2006; Jazzar & Algozzine, 2007), our findings indicate that the relationships created by the leader, the philosophies and structures that s/he supports, and the decisions that s/he makes will influence the entire school. With this in mind, the leader must consciously and intentionally take the actions that s/he believes are in the best interests of the students, while modeling the importance of caring and just relationships and understanding that his/her decisions have consequences across the entire system. For example, the city's dynamics of social and cultural norms (i.e., its being sharply segregated along racial lines) seem to have played a role in how formal school leaders failed to build trust and communicate with staff, students, and community. There was an absence of what Johnston (1997) views as a process of envisioning and achieving what might be, which involves the ability and desire to dialogue and critique for the common good. Doing this will afford the leader the opportunity to collaborate with all the stakeholders in a democratic learning community (Furman, 2004), ensuring that the school will reflect the community's intended goals—to assist all students in fully realizing their potential, with the understanding that they are connected to others through a web of interrelationships of which they may not even be conscious, but one that exists nonetheless.

Examining distributed leadership in the context of a school begins to describe ways formal and informal leaders (i.e., leaders and followers, at times reciprocal) develop an understanding of and engage in social justice. At DuBois High School, leaders, followers, and situations interacted in ways that developed over time to form distinct forms and patterns of leadership practice. These leadership practices were dynamic and revolutionary, in that educators who led as transformational public intellectuals in one situation were then followers when practicing "bridge" leadership. Put differently, in this study, leadership for social justice was distributed in a fluid manner that evolved over time and varied as it was practiced by various leaders and followers in different situations.

As Freire (1989) asserts, all human beings perform as transformative public intellectuals by constantly interpreting and giving meaning to the world and participating in a particular conception of the world. At DuBois, both administrators and teachers at times could be touted as transformative public intellectuals who combined scholarly reflection and practice in the service of educating students to be thoughtful, active citizens (Giroux, 1988; Larson & Murtadha, 2002; Sernak, 2006). Whether it was the subcommunity of scholars in the IB program who engaged one another and students in critical dialogues about social justice, the school's Black leaders (formal and informal) who felt a moral obligation to be role models to students and in the Black community, or the less outspoken teacher who in a more subtle way (i.e., classroom dialogues and activities) addressed issues of inequities, they all were activists initiating soft or hard revolutions to change the conditions of the students they served. They had become more aware of equity issues and had developed their critical consciousness toward equity issues. While these assertions were promising, many of these same potential leaders for social justice had difficulty making the transition from awareness to action. Yet, these educators and leaders paid attention to the "silenced voice" of marginalized students to impact school policies that sometimes create inequities (Mitra, 2006; Scheurich & Skrla, 2003; Shoho, Merchant, & Lugg, 2005). Both formal and informal leaders committed to this ideal grappled with how to advocate for social justice when the climate and structure of DuBois made it nearly impossible to do so.

At times, both formal and informal leaders were constrained by the organizational context because there was ambiguity about how to address issues of social justice that directly and indirectly had an impact on students, and on teaching and learning more broadly construed. Many leaders had to consciously strategize individually and/or collectively to find ways to dismantle the structural barriers at DuBois in pursuit of social justice. Still, these leaders inspired commitment and action and led as peer problem solvers who built broad-based involvement. Above all, these leaders intended to sustain hope and participation by capitalizing on the need for overall improved communication and awareness of the issue. Essentially, DuBois school leaders brought theoretical knowledge and ethical behaviors to the test of practicality, confronting organizational and/or institutional barriers to promoting social justice, and learned to work with extant notions regarding social justice activity (Brooks & Normore, 2005).

The findings from this study have clear implications for the practice and preparation of educational leaders, as they suggest that leadership for social justice, as a practiced phenomenon, is ripe with promise, but also fraught with complexity and contradiction. Further, approaching the study of distributed leadership by supplementing it with complementary analytic concepts enriches our understanding of a promising and developing theory. Approaching leadership for social justice concepts from a distributed perspective helps shed light on the dynamic nature of these concepts. Leadership bridgework, critical activism, and transformational public intellectualism seem to be stretched over the school in a manner that is influenced by the interactions of leaders and followers, as they shift and develop from situation to situation and over time. This means that leadership for social justice, as conceptualized in this manner, is dynamic and protean. It is a fluid phenomenon that does not necessarily reside in superhero leaders who inspire those around them to rise up against inequity, but it instead may be something practiced *between* leaders and followers, mediated by the tools and routines that provide structure (and sometimes confusion) to these interactions and the ways in which leaders, followers, and situations evolve over time in a particular context (Donaldson, 2006).

HOW CAN DISTRIBUTED LEADERSHIP FOR SOCIAL JUSTICE IMPROVE EDUCATION?

In terms of educational leadership preparation and training, it seems important to consider that if leaders intend to influence the future of social justice, they need to focus on re-evaluating the socialization experiences, both formal and informal, to determine how these experiences have helped or dissuaded them from promoting social justice issues as educational leaders. Such a reflection and discussion bring to light the practical applications, actionable strategies, and sharing of effective practices that educators might readily implement in their work. Focusing on problems they are facing, triumphs they have experienced might help inform the way educational leaders are prepared and socialized regarding issues of social justice in the workplace. Preparation programs ought to include in their curriculum opportunities for preservice administrators to engage in discourse that will raise awareness about social justice and develop the knowledge and disposition to eradicate injustices perpetuated in policies and practices. In support of Starratt (2004) and Merchant and Shoho (2006), such a discourse can lead to proactive responsibility, personal and professional authenticity, and an affirming, critical, and enabling presence to the workers and the work involved in leading, teaching, and learning at all levels of education.

CHAPTER 3

Black Leadership, White Leadership: Race and Race Relations in an Urban High School

As Brown (2005) observed, "Schools in a racially diverse society will require leaders and models of leadership that will address the racial, cultural, and ethnic makeup of the school community" (p. 585). However, while researchers during the past several decades have begun to investigate and interrogate the complicated dynamics of race and school leadership (e.g., Bryant, 1998; Capper, 1993; Dantley, 2005; López, 2003; Tillman, 2002), these issues remain among the largest elephants in the schoolhouse about which few practitioners or scholars will speak (Wynne, 1999). Moreover, as many of the studies cited above focused on issues of race, it is important to point out that Brown's quote above addresses racial *diversity* and not only race; inquiry is needed both in the area of race and school leadership, and also in the area of race *relations* and school leadership.

The purpose of this chapter was to investigate how race and race relations influence school leadership practice. More specifically, it was to identify cultural norms and beliefs within and between racial leadership subcultures of a single school. The chapter centers on a conceptual framework that drew on race and race relation research in educational leadership, and from an anthropological approach called moiety cultural analysis (Wolcott, 2003). When a culture (in this case, the school's culture) is conceptualized in this manner, it is conceived as comprising two distinct and separate subcultures that operate and interact in particular ways. These subcultures could be based on racial, gender, organizational, or any other number of distinguishing cultural distinctions, depending on the values and emphases of particular cultures. In this case, given findings suggested by preliminary data analysis and the cultural context of the setting, the school's culture was conceptually split into two racial leadership subcultures, one Black and one White. Two questions guided fieldwork and analyses:

37

1. How do the cultural norms and beliefs of each of the two racial leadership subcultures influence members' leadership practice?
2. How do the subcultures interact, with respect to anthropological findings that interaction of two subcultures is characterized by antithesis, rivalry, reciprocity, and complementarity?

SCHOOL LEADERSHIP AS A RACIAL MOIETY

Research on race and school leadership in the United States has focused on the styles and personal experiences of "minority" leaders, on White racism and White privilege, and on antiracism, and is treated as a subconstruct in studies focused on democratic leadership, ethics, social justice, and equity (Bryant, 1998; Gooden, 2005; Grogan, 1999; Larson & Murtadha, 2002; Shapiro & Stefkovich, 2001; Starratt, 1997; Young & Laible, 2000). Many works in these lines of inquiry are conceptually rich and suggest innovative strategies for preparing educational leaders and for transforming leadership practice into a force for justice that serves students equitably (Marshall & Oliva, 2006). However, while these possibilities are exciting and inspiring, there is a need to explore and refine such notions through investigation at the school site level and, ultimately, in a variety of communities of educational leadership practice. For example, Gooden (2005) lamented that in leadership literature on U.S. schools, there remains a tremendous gap in the knowledge base concerning Black school leadership. He noted that while useful and thorough studies have documented the leadership practice of African American superintendents (e.g., Alston, 1999), there is a relatively paltry corpus of work focused on Black school leaders. Brown (2005) agreed and further argued for the "need to investigate school administration in specific social, political, and racial contexts" (p. 587). This research seeks to make a contribution to race relations literature in school leadership by exploring the way racial leadership subcultures interact in an urban school setting.

Researchers also suggest that understanding norms and beliefs is at the core of a school's leadership culture (Fullan, 2001; Hargreaves, 1993; Yukl, 1998). Yet Schein (1992) noted an important gap in this literature when he observed that "there is a growing issue surrounding diversity and the possibility that different racial groups . . . are forming subcultures around their particular career concerns" (p. 274).

The moiety technique allows for a culture to be conceived of and described as two distinct subcultures. In this case, the overarching unit of cultural analysis was the school's culture, and given the unique demographics of the setting, the two subcultures comprised "Black" leaders and "White" leaders (see Figure 3.1). Research on moieties suggests certain ways that such subcultures interact, and these concepts also guided our analysis.

When conducting research on a moiety system, anthropologists seek to explore each subculture, in and of itself, and then investigate the dynamics of interaction between the two. While an understanding of each subculture yields interesting insights, the real benefit of moiety analysis lies in its potential to help explain complex social systems (Schusky, 1972). Moiety subcultures interact in four distinct modes: (1) They interact with *antithesis* when values and behaviors of the subcultures come into conflict; (2) They interact through *rivalry* when the two sides engage in sociopolitical struggles for control of institutional processes and products; (3) They interact with *reciprocity*, indicated by "give-and-take" social exchanges, which might be transactional and/or transformational; (4) They interact *complementarily*, when each half of the moiety assumes differentiated functions in order to achieve organizational goals. While many studies have investigated school leadership culture (Deal & Peterson, 1999), and a few have used moiety analysis (Wolcott, 2003), no studies have used

Figure 3.1. A Moiety of Two Racial Subcultures

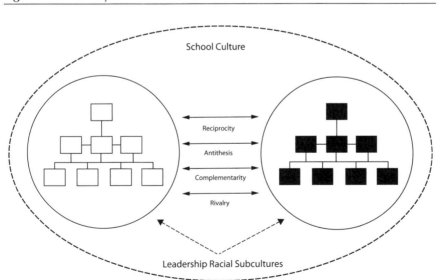

the technique to explore issues of race and race relations among leaders in schools. The following sections explore how these concepts looked at DuBois High School.

BLACK LEADERSHIP SUBCULTURE AT DuBOIS HIGH SCHOOL

The Black school leaders, who included the principal, assistant principal for curriculum, dean of students, athletic director, several department chairs, and even more teacher leaders, had particular behavioral and attitudinal expectations of themselves and of other subculture members. Analysis of data suggested three themes that collectively characterized these dynamics: (1) respect for differentiated gender roles among Black school leaders; (2) a need to serve students and the community as role models and advocates; and (3) a fear that the predominantly White district leadership, and White leaders within the school, were not committed to Black students.

Differentiated Gender Roles Among Black School Leaders

Among the Black leaders at DuBois High School, the leadership activities of women and men were markedly different. While Black men generally held higher positions of formal authority in the school, women routinely functioned as a "moral compass" for day-to-day leadership decisions. For example, on one occasion a table of Black school leaders sat eating lunch. The four men at the table included the principal, dean of students, and two veteran teachers. The lone woman at the table, the school's head administrative assistant, joined the group halfway through the meal. The men were discussing an African American sophomore boy who had come to school that day dressed in women's clothes, or, as one of the veteran teachers giddily repeated: "The boy's dressed up like a faggot." The men joked at the student's expense for more than 10 minutes, and all but the man who called the boy a faggot referred to him as a "sissy." They offered their opinions about which students would "beat that sissy down 'til he leaked." In local parlance, "leaked" is slang for bleeding. When the administrative assistant joined the discussion, she listened silently for a few minutes, and then began shaking her head in disapproval. This barely visible gesture had the effect of causing all of the men to stop speaking. At that point she interjected:

> Sissy? What kind of talk is that? Where'd you all ever learn to use that word? He's *gay* or he's *homosexual*, or maybe he just wants to

dress that way. That boy has a right to wear what he wants to wear and do what he wants to do. If he's gay, we should protect him if he's in danger of getting beat down. I'm proud of him for doing what he's doing. He's got a lot of guts to wear that skirt to school. You men ought to be ashamed of yourselves for talking like this.

The men fell silent, and eventually the principal explained that of course she was right, they had to protect the student if he was in danger. There were many other instances like this that suggested deference to differentiated gender roles among Black leaders, especially in regard to the moral dynamics of situations. Black women, even if they occupied a position of lesser formal authority, commonly would admonish Black male leaders for "not doing what was right" and assume important informal leadership roles. By and large, these Black male leaders capitulated when challenged in this manner.

Black Leaders as Role Models and Advocates

As one guidance counselor explained, "I am a role model and advocate for Black kids and the Black community." Many Black school leaders, male and female, explained the importance of presenting a professional image while on the job so that, as one reading coach explained, "they understand that men can be more than rappers and drug dealers and women don't need to be a hoochie mama to get attention and respect." Black leaders, formal and informal, often spoke of the uphill battle they constantly waged against popular culture, and about how they crafted many school policies to dissuade students from expressing themselves in violent or deviant ways. For example, the maxim on the lips of all school leaders about the school's dress code was: "no bud, no booze, no gats." Students wearing clothes displaying any of these (drugs, liquor, or guns) were made to wear large t-shirts that featured the school crest until they could change into acceptable clothes. Black leaders were, as a group, the most professionally dressed group of leaders on campus (i.e., men commonly wore a suit and tie, while women dressed in business attire).

But projecting a professional image was only part of the work. As one teacher leader noted, "Style is one thing but I want to be more for these kids than a sharp suit." Black leaders worked as advocates for students and, importantly, for their Black leadership peers. In many instances, Black leaders would spread the word about scholarship opportunities, academic support, and other resources available to struggling students, most (but not all) of whom were African American students. Black school leaders, especially the principal, also actively recruited

Black teachers to the school and helped mentor promising Black teachers into formal leadership positions. Among Black school leaders, there was a strong esprit de corps and sense of camaraderie among those who held positions such as department chairs, assistant principals, and other formal positions.

Fear and Mistrust of White Colleagues and a District "Leadership Lynch Mob"

Black leaders at DuBois often expressed fear that the predominantly White district leadership, and White leaders at the district level, were not committed to supporting Black students or their Black educational colleagues. It was striking that nearly every district representative who visited the school during the course of the school year was White, and that they came mainly for ceremonial occasions or to carry a reprimand rather than visiting to offer support or constructive counsel. When such "district visits" were planned, the principal would whip the staff into a preparatory frenzy in an effort to, as he said, "put on a good face for the district." This included email messages wherein the principal would exhort teachers to be on their best behavior and to dress professionally. As the dean of students explained, calls from the central office were usually to deliver threats and punishment, and many other Black school leaders explained that they didn't think administrators at the district level wanted DuBois to succeed. It was a commonly held belief among Black school leaders that the reason the school was open was, as a veteran teacher explained, to provide a "dumping ground for the kids no one else wants. It's a dumping ground for the Black kids." The same teacher—greatly respected as a leader at the school site—suggested that if the school ever did start having success, the district was likely to send out a "lynch mob" that would undo their work and/or "fire us all." When this perception was presented to other Black leaders in the school, they agreed that this was a very real possibility.

WHITE LEADERSHIP SUBCULTURE AT DuBOIS HIGH SCHOOL

White school leaders, including the assistant principal for facilities, assistant principal for attendance and discipline, and academic magnet program coordinator; a few department chairs; and several veteran teacher leaders had a distinctly different set of cultural values than Black school leaders. Data collected while exploring members' behaviors and attitudes among the school's White leadership subculture suggested the following themes: (a) respect for, and deference to, a patriarchal, male-dominated vision of leadership; (b) a paradoxical sense that institutional rewards, and student achievement, were based on merit *and* the influence of a preferential "good ol' boys network"; and (c) a belief that the values and attitudes of Black students and their families ultimately would prevent many of them from finding success in school or in life.

Father Knows Best: Gender and White Leadership

White school leaders at DuBois showed respect for, and deference to, a patriarchal, male-dominated vision of leadership. Women with greater experience, and even with greater positional power than their male colleagues, often deferred to men when decisions had to be made. As one veteran teacher, who is a woman, commented:

> I learned a long time ago that a woman's place is in the classroom, not in the principal's office . . . at least in this school. I find that when I speak up to the school's leaders they don't listen. They have a way of doing things that privileges a forceful and at times scary type of leadership. All muscle and no brains. I think it has to do with White administrators working in a Black school. They are afraid of a culture they don't understand so they go on the offensive and forget about nurturing and making a personal connection. I can't be bothered by all that nonsense, so I shut my door and act as a leader in my classroom.

This gender deference among White leaders was evident in both interpersonal exchanges and group settings. It was common to observe White women—some of whom were tremendously gifted and assertive instructional and curriculum leaders in their classrooms and departments—capitulating to men's direction and dicta regularly when it came to extra-instructional and school-wide issues.

Hard Work and Who You Know:
White Leaders' Perspectives on the Keys to Success

White school leaders professed a widespread belief in the paradox that both institutional rewards and student achievement were based on individual merit *and* the influence of a preferential "good ol' boys network." White leaders commonly explained that Black students scored poorly on achievement examinations because, as one White teacher explained, "they don't care. They have a culture that doesn't value education. They don't have books at home and their parents didn't graduate from high school so they don't care if their kids do." These racial stereotypes and general-izations were common, and alarmingly supported and unquestioned by many teachers with cryptic references to, as an assistant principal said, "scientific research that shows these race things are true." No White leader who made such a claim could ever produce any of this research or remem-ber the name of the studies ostensibly read.

While describing the cultural disadvantage their Black students faced, White school leaders also would explain that the reason many White stu-dents, teachers, and administrators succeeded was because of the influ-ence of a systemic elite that promoted and protected White people in general, but especially White people of influence. To a person, White lead-ers suggested that, as one teacher explained, "the good ol' boys network is alive and well, both in the school system and in the community." For example, one teacher explained how a local legislator's daughter miracu-lously graduated even though she had failed his class, which was required as part of the core curriculum. "I don't know exactly what happened, but I know that the grade I submitted would have prevented her graduation and I know that daddy made a phone call." Similarly, all three assistant principals explained that hiring practices in the district were heavily in-fluenced both by, as one said, "race and by who you know." This was corroborated by district personnel data, which showed that Black school leaders were much more likely to be placed at Black schools.

White Leaders and the Belief of Social Reproduction

While not all White school leaders suggested as much, a majority es-poused a belief that the values and attitudes of Black students and their families ultimately would prevent many of them from finding success in school or in life. They explained that this was due to social and cul-tural processes beyond an educator's control. White leaders commonly explained that many students had, as a veteran teacher explained, "too many things working against them that would ultimately undo their po-tential" to succeed. To White leaders, although few ever said that they had visited a Black student's home, this meant that students went home to latchkey homes, broken families, incarcerated parents, or no parents at all. From White leaders' perspectives, Black students had little academic support, and many faced poverty that prevented them from having ba-sic necessities. While this very well could have been the case, almost no White leaders said they had ever been to visit a student at home and few suggested they had had any kind of substantive conversations about chal-lenges or opportunities students might have had for success. Most White leaders at the school looked at Black students and saw stereotypes that were beyond their ability to influence.

DUAL CULTURE INTERACTION AT DuBOIS HIGH SCHOOL

In keeping with anthropological moiety literature, patterns emerged that suggested the two subcultures interacted in terms of antithesis, rivalry, reciprocity, and complementarity.

Antithesis and Rivalry

There was mutual distrust between Black school leaders and White school leaders, and this lack of trust was "stretched over" formal and informal forms of leadership at all levels of the school organization. Leaders in both moieties described their relations with the other moiety as professional, but not personal. As the dean of students explained, "We do our jobs and then drive back to our neighborhoods. Some of us drive home to the Black neighborhoods and some drive home to White homes." Informally, it was common for leaders in either moiety to abruptly stop a conversation as soon as a member of the other moiety entered a room. Likewise, leaders would often code-switch as soon as a member of the other moiety arrived on the scene and enter into a seemingly innocuous conversation using bland "leaderspeak" when they might have been engaged in an important school-related conversation only a few seconds before. For example, on one occasion, two White assistant principals were discussing how one teacher, who happened to be African American, was remiss in turning in her attendance reports in a timely manner. As they discussed ways they might "fix the situation," the African American principal walked into the room and asked what they were discussing. "Facilities," they said almost in unison. Later, one of the assistant principals explained that "if [the principal] heard us talking about [the teacher], he would have said we were criticizing her because she is Black. He always pulls the race card." This nondialogic dynamic impacted countless conversations among the school's leaders. This dynamic was likewise supported by several Black leaders in the school, one of whom suggested that "you gotta talk like the Black folks when they're around and like the White folks when you're around them. You can't talk about race with the White folks; they don't get it—and they misinterpret genuine conversation as aggression."

Reciprocity

Relationships between Black school leaders and White school leaders were generally transactional rather than transformational. This was evident in many settings and situations. When moiety members interacted with nonmoiety members, there was often what an assistant principal and several teachers described as a "what-can-you-do-for-me?"

attitude that was clearly absent when the same members interacted with in-moiety members. While White leaders tended to be annoyed by this form of between-moiety interaction, Black leaders accepted it as a social norm that both protected them and ensured that they were "not being used just for nothing," as the dean of students suggested. Within-moiety exchanges were more commonly transformational and focused on personal and professional forms of support and camaraderie that advanced members' interests and contributed to goal attainment.

Complementarity

The two halves of the moiety typically would compromise and complement each other with respect to the formal educational work of the school, such as development of the School Improvement Plan, but came to silent agreement on other issues. Black school leaders and White school leaders engaged, apparently by mutual consent, in a "conspiracy of silence" and refrained from acknowledging, discussing, or engaging issues of race with one another. White school leaders tended to dismiss issues of race as issues of class, while Black school leaders refrained from discussing issues of race with their White colleagues, since they saw no safe forum in which they could broach the subject. Further, several Black leaders explained that White leaders "could never understand" race and racism the way they did, so there was no reason to initiate a dialogue.

White school leaders' strategy of shifting the topic from race to class enabled them to avoid uncomfortable conversations with one another and with their Black colleagues. White leaders commonly explained, as did this teacher, that a few examples here and there were evidence that class, and not race, was the operational issue.

> I know this one African American kid whose father is a doctor and mother is a lawyer. The kid drives a nicer car than I do and he speaks perfect English, not all that ghetto slang. He does great in school. So, I think it's more about coming from a family that doesn't have those ghetto values. It isn't about race, it's about class.

White school leaders at DuBois would use examples like this as evidence that class mattered more than race. This allowed them to conveniently ignore the "lower-class" students who made up 85% of the school's population by not giving them additional resources, feedback, or assistance—"they" were beyond help.

The bottom line is that DuBois was effectively two schools, divided by race. The White school leaders had their own culture; the Black school leaders had another culture, and they interacted in certain ways, employ-ing informal yet powerful rules of behavior. In some cases, it seems like allegiance to one's race meant more to many of these educators than a commitment to student learning. Yet, while this is perhaps dispiriting, it is also important to note that within each of the cultures there were transfor-mational practices where leaders helped and assisted one another. Sadly, when races interacted, this was not often the case, as a culture of mistrust prevailed.

Part II

RACISM AND EDUCATIONAL MISLEADERSHIP

Honky Leadership:
White Teacher in a
Black School

Dalton Conley's (2000) memoir *Honky* tells the tale of growing up White in a Black and Hispanic neighborhood in Manhattan. Through the eyes of a child, we watch as Conley loses his racial innocence and understands issues such as social class, race, racism, and White privilege long before he ever hears the terms. Yet while he recalls his early years as something close to blissful ignorance, he notes the point when an important transition occurred:

> By then I had learned that I was white and other people around me weren't, but I had yet to understand what that difference meant. I had yet to learn the privileges that attended whiteness. One month in public school would fix all that. (p. 42)

School showed Conley that he was taught differently than his Black and Hispanic peers, was disciplined differently, was spoken to differently, had a different set of expectations and a special set of informal rules, and that the consequences for missteps in school were not as serious for him as for students of color. He was White—he was privileged. Conley learned that "racial groupings were about domination and struggles for power . . . and that racial barriers were taken as both natural and insurmountable" (p. 49). *Honky* chronicles Conley's awakening; it is the journey from ignorance to recognition of the role of race in American society. Unfortunately, few educators make this journey.

This chapter, painfully at times, presents data gleaned from four separate interviews I conducted with a single teacher, Dustin, who never experienced the kind of awareness and awakening about race that Conley underwent. What you are about to read is a narrative that exudes uncritical White privilege, a complete lack of respect for students' culture, and indeed a great deal of contempt for the profession of teaching.

*   *   *

I walked into Dustin's room. In many ways, his was a typical high school classroom at DuBois. The paint needed a fresh coat, there were stacks of paper scattered over his desk, and a collage of institutional art and student work appeared on the walls. I settled into a student desk and began by casually asking him about how things were going. He let out a long, exaggerated sigh.

"So, this year's been the most stressful for me, it's like Aaaaah! You know, I just have to let it go because my kids suck this time around. There's just no calming them down. It's crazy."

"How do you mean?" I asked. "What's different?"

"Well, I got some time off and recharged my batteries. You know, I had a chance to forget about this place and these kids. You need to do that—get away from all this and just be yourself. The best thing about being a teacher is all the days off. I just realized the other day I'm going to have a 4-day week—no, a 3-day week, 'cause of President's Day. With teacher planning days coming up, that means I had a 3-day week, another 3-day week, and then 4-day week, and then it's spring break. It's awesome!"

"Doesn't that get in the way of instruction?" I wondered.

"Ha!" Dustin laughed off my question. We met during his planning period and his room was empty. He leaned back in his chair and put his feet up on a student desk in the front row. "On top of that, all I did the past 2 weeks was administer the state test. It went fine. I missed one of the days. As far as how my students did, most of them will fail. I mean, look at this school's report card! We're working with the weakest students you can imagine. But, let me go through the classes in my head and see what I think. My reading students . . . they don't call it that, but it's all remedial—all Black—I am pretty confident they'll do pretty well this time around. Of course, when I say pretty well I don't mean *good*, like what *good* would be to you and me, I mean good for *them*. Those kids couldn't read when they showed up and I'm not a miracle worker. They'll fail, but their scores should go up."

"So, you think they've made progress?" I asked.

"No. They haven't made progress. I'm just an optimist. Seriously, their culture doesn't value education. No books at home. No computer. Parents who can't read, and who don't give a crap about school. These kids only care about baggy pants, rap music, basketball, and football. The way I see it, my job is to introduce them to our culture—hell, it's probably the only culture they'll ever get in their lifetime. I need to make sure they understand who Shakespeare was. That's the kind of thing that educated people know—you know? Last year I taught *Othello* and *Taming of the Shrew,* and I did a great job with it, but they hated it. I even showed an episode of

Moonlighting that was all based on *Taming of the Shrew* and they didn't even know what *Moonlighting* was! It was ridiculous. Like, who doesn't know Bruce Willis? So this year I tried *Romeo and Juliet*, and I showed the version that Leonardo DiCaprio did, *Romeo + Juliet*. They didn't get that either. They're stupid. You have to know that stuff to get through college."

"I never watched *Moonlighting*," I said. "Maybe these kids didn't either. And, wasn't it on before they were born?"

"Hm," Dustin thought, "maybe."

"I never saw that DiCaprio flick, either," I said.

"Anyway, this is the fourth time I've had my reading students take the test, and I feel more confident this time than any of the other three. So that's good. I got old copies of the test and we just answered the questions over and over. I had them look it all up. I'm sure it will help. And then my 9th- and 10th-graders, if they don't take it seriously, then they're just not gonna pass. And believe me, most of those kids don't take it seriously. They're like, YO! They can't even speak without mumbling. I mean, can you understand what these kids are saying?"

"So, you're using old copies of the test to get them ready?" I asked. "No wonder they're grumbling, I would too!"

Dustin laughed.

"Well, it's all about motivation and support, that's really what I've found. It's always the kids that say to themselves, 'I'm not gonna let this happen to me,' that say, 'No! I won't accept the fact that my culture is ridiculous and my parents and friends would rather sell crack than study. I'm gonna get out of here!' They're the ones that pass. The ones who have a chance. It happens that way every time."

"So, you think that peer support is important?" I asked. "That makes a lot of sense."

Dustin thought for a moment. "Well maybe, but it's like the dumb get dumber. You know how people say that success brings more success? Well, failure also breeds more failure. Some kids in my intensive reading class feel bad about themselves and get into a downward spiral, 'Oh, I don't know how to do it.' Or they think it's cool not to read things—have you ever heard anything so *stupid*? I tell them that if they don't learn to read Shakespeare they'll only need to know how to read the instructions on the McDonald's French fry machine. I tell them I like my fries cooked properly when I go through the drive-through! They think that's funny."

"They do? That sounds awful."

"No, man, you have to be there—it's hilarious!" Dustin chuckled. He continued. "We started this new program, this 15 minutes of reading thing. For me, it's cool—the requirement is no instruction at all during that time. You're supposed to model good reading behavior so I sit and read a book. But these kids, they don't like to be forced to do stuff. The program keeps changing, which is really stupid in my opinion. First it was just reading—anything you like. Then when we got a reading coach, it became 'use a journal.' Then it was 'don't use a journal, only reading.' Now, it's reading and taking notes; at one point they changed it from reading anything you want to reading test-prep items. I don't think the administration has its act together. I've been doing whatever I want anyway. I'd imagine a lot of teachers are just doing whatever. There's probably a bunch of teachers who just don't have them do anything, or they just use it as class time. I've finally gotten them, most of them, to actually start reading every day at this point. So that's better, I think, than trying to have them do all the reading coach's little activities. I was always told that you get better at reading by reading." He paused, then started again.

"Here's how I do it: I decided to start grading them on whether they read or not. And, as a part of class, I walk around and see what they brought to class. At first most of them just put their heads down and slept so I took away points. Now they realize they can bring in anything they want to read. One kid who can barely read finally brought a Spider Man comic book today. I'm like, 'Yay!' I showed the whole class—'Look, ShaQuan brought a book!' They thought it was really funny. I'm good with the kids. They all bring something they like. That's fine, I say, read a comic book. At least it was Spider Man—that's *our* culture, so maybe there's a value to it. Bring a donut wrapper. I don't care. That's fine."

"Really," I asked, "you said that to the whole class?"

"Yep," Dustin said. His eyes were beaming, and while I was getting increasingly disgusted with him I realized he was proud of his teaching style. He was sure he was doing the right thing by belittling students and embarrassing them in front of their peers. He continued.

"But here's the thing with our scores, our school grade. It's really terrible 'cause we dropped a letter grade and that makes everyone look incompetent. It reflects badly on the kids, the school, the community, on everyone. The reading scores didn't improve. They didn't get worse, but they didn't improve. I thought that was pretty good, but the state says we have to show 'gains.' They clearly don't see what I have to work with when I come to school every day.

"Because of our school grade, we had all these crisis meetings—all these 'what-are-we-going-to-do' meetings. We would talk about this stuff we could do. When we all know there's nothing we can do with this student population. Everybody's sort of uncomfortable and on thin ice and we'd eventually agree on something just to get out of the meeting. Well, it's like this. Certain people have these ideas, and then other people have these ideas. It just goes on and on. Some people didn't like it, some people did, but the bottom line is that I never heard anything more about it and I've not changed a thing I've done in my classroom unless I get bored.

"It's always like that. You sit in those meetings and everyone gets excited but nothing ever changes. I think the problem with all this is that there isn't any consistency. Maybe there's a curriculum at the state level. I think there is, actually. I know there are standards we're supposed to follow but have you seen them?"

"I have seen them," I said.

Dustin responded with sarcasm. "So they do exist! They're really like college preparatory in nature, right? In any event they're completely irrelevant in this school. How about a class like 'Hip-Hop Mumbling' or 'Ghetto Grammar'? Those would be useful! Instead of things like how to identify a gerund, we need to teach these kids real-life skills like how to fill out a McDonald's application. Seriously, you might think that sounds harsh, but most of these kids won't make it out of the ghetto."

"Why do you think that is?" I asked.

Dustin started in again. "Sometimes they complain about what I teach. 'Oh, I did this 2 years ago' and blah, blah, blah, but I tell them they must be lying because they still can't do whatever it is! I do think we're sort of running out of material. But it's a lot of work because you have to actually see where the kids are. They say they did stuff in the past, but they can't tell me anything about it—they say they did *Julius Caesar* but they can't tell me the plot. They tell me they did *Lear* but they think it's funny when I say Goneril because it sounds like gonorrhea. They laugh and I tell them they're idiots if they laugh at Shakespeare. Shakespeare is our culture, after all. I mean, he wasn't American, obviously, but it's our culture. It's the culture of educated people in this country. You know what I mean?

"Anyway, about the tests. They're still sort of compiling the results for everything and stuff like that. I've been told every year that I would see data for my classroom—data that would tell me where I should focus and what worked and what didn't, but that's never happened. There isn't a lot of follow-up to make sure that everybody is doing what they are supposed to be doing. There are always a lot of meetings. And everybody says, 'Okay, this is what we're gonna do,' but whether that actually happened, whether it ever happens, I have no idea. I know there are a few things I didn't do. But as far as the accountability thing goes, I do it myself with the grades I give to my students."

Dustin leaned forward and became very serious. "I think it's my responsibility to society to fail kids who can't read. We need kids to work at fast food places, at Wal-Mart, and at gas stations. Grades ultimately are success—with them you have a chance and without them you'll be bagging groceries, if you're lucky. Sometimes I feel bad that all these Black kids fail, but it's not my fault. It's really hopeless trying to teach them."

"Maybe you could try different methods. Maybe they can't relate to Shakespeare," I responded. He misinterpreted my suggestion that his teaching was culturally irrelevant as a validation that, indeed, the students deserved to fail.

"Exactly! See? I think the place I've really improved since I started teaching is in discipline. I'm handling my students better. Before, I would write a referral. Not much would happen except that the kid would resent me for it and the administrators saw it as a hassle. One kid even told me I was racist because I only referred Black kids. Well, I said, the simple truth is that Black kids are the troublemakers in this school. It's just a coincidence, I said. I'm definitely not racist, of course. One of my best friends is Black! I like LL Cool J. I know that's not PC but the truth is that Black kids have crappy attitudes and they aren't here to learn. I'm sort of at the point now where I'm not really needing to write referrals; I just tell those kids to put their heads down and go to sleep if they hate the class. It works well—they aren't going to learn anything anyway, and I'm not pestering the administrators."

"You tell them it's okay to go to sleep?"

"Genius, huh?" Dustin tapped his temple to show that he was smart. "It's really helped me to let go of the things I can't change and to focus on what I love about teaching, these great books. Just not letting it get to me as much has helped me enjoy being a teacher much more. I really have a more positive attitude since I realized that the kids' success is not my responsibility—I can't change their destiny and it isn't my job to do that. If they decide to learn, I'll teach them. If they don't care, I'm obligated to give them a seat in the classroom since this is public education but I'm not obligated to force education on people who don't want it. You know, I've noticed the days when I'm in a bad mood I have bad classes. Days when I'm in a good mood I have good classes. So, that's one of the biggest things, I've grown to the point where I realize that I have to take care of myself first and worry about the kids after that. You have to just sort of let things go a little bit to survive in a school like this. Working here is a compromise. If it works well, they come up a little bit to my level and I come down a little bit in terms of my expectations. It's realistic that way. We can just get by, I guess I would say."

"So, you've found success by lowering your expectations?" I asked.

"Well, you could say it that way, but I'd rather say I'm meeting them where they are. Look, Jeff, the main problem is that I see the majority of these students several times. They'll have a regular reading class their first year and fail. Then, I have them in remedial classes the other years. And so, they've all seen my material before. We ought to buy other stuff, maybe next year we'll have to buy something else but I'm comfortable with my stuff so I teach it. I just tell the kids that they're only in those classes because they failed, so obviously they didn't get it the first time around. I'm sure it's boring for them to listen to the same stuff every year, but that's their choice—failure—I didn't take the tests for them. It isn't my problem.

"And, I have no idea what they go home to. That's not true, I have an idea. I have an idea because I drive past the projects on my way to school every day, you know? It's poverty, man, real poverty. It's a part of the city I try to avoid, I mean, I wouldn't want to be out in this school's neighborhoods after dark. Especially since I know what these kids are like! It isn't safe. And I didn't see that when I was in high school. I'm a different generation than these children, and I didn't grow up around here. I grew up in a completely different culture. It was the suburbs of Boston. And there were maybe one or two kids in the school who didn't care about school. Here, I have classes filled with them. It makes me angry that they don't see school as an opportunity to get out of those crappy neighborhoods—it's like they want to be there, they're okay with it—maybe they're resigned to their fate.

"And some of them could do it, a few kids I have in every class are really smart. Those kids are even worse! They make me more angry because they're really smart and they kind of do stuff sometimes, but they still flunk in the end because they're too busy being distracted or screwing around with stuff that isn't important.

"To give you an example, I have one kid whose mom called this morning and said that I can't let him sit next to so-and-so because it's too distracting. Today, he's doing better 'cause I talked to him and said, 'Hey, your mom called today, and this is what we have to do. We can't do this anymore.' He said all right. Well, he actually said something that sounded like *a-yeet!* All right, all right—they all say all right, but then they do the same damned things again and again. And that's what makes me so angry. But his mom is calling, at least. That happens very seldom. Mostly they don't care about education. Mostly the mothers are working two jobs and the father is in jail, or at least not at home."

"Hm," I said. "Don't you think that's a stereotype?"

"No. It's reality." Dustin thought for a moment, then started again. "Because you're so isolated you get lonely, but because you're so isolated, everyone leaves you alone. You can kind of do whatever you want. Nobody is looking over your shoulder. That is what I love about the job, I come in and nobody's here. It's just me. Which is nice, but if I were not, in my humble opinion, a good teacher like I am, and I was just slacking off and the kids weren't doing anything, nobody would know for a long time. I'm not sure they would ever know, to be honest.

"Let me tell you something about the disconnect between us teachers and the administrators around here. I recently had my evaluation. You're supposed to have three a year, but I've only had one the whole time I've taught here. Anyway, for my single evaluation I received an email from the principal's secretary and I was asked to make an appointment. Of course, I wanted to have a full lesson so I could do my thing, so I could show him what I'm doing. It was supposed to be on a Tuesday, but he showed up on Monday, a day early! Based on where the students were for that particular class on that particular day, I decided not to change it. All we were doing was working on a review worksheet and so, I thought, 'He's coming in, but you know what, it's too bad.' I mean, it's not exactly what I wanted, but I thought, okay, I'll be helping the students directly with their work. I was trying to help them understand something in *Romeo and Juliet*. So the principal came in, and he sat at my desk as I walked around the room. It felt a little funny that he was sitting at my desk. He looked so bored! He left 5 minutes before class ended and didn't say a word to me. I saw him write some stuff down at the very beginning of the class but then he just stared out the window. He was vacant. I ignored him because I didn't want to see if he was watching me. If he's watching me, fine, I'm just going to do my thing. So I'm walking around the room the entire period helping the students out individually. About a week later, he sent an email stating that—and I don't agree with this at all—but, stating that from what I did in the class he wasn't able to evaluate me. I can agree with that on one level; of course you can't really evaluate a teacher when the kids are doing independent work. But, if he was looking for certain strategies, they were happening, just not in front of the class. A few days later he sent an email out to the entire school saying that we weren't supposed to only do worksheets with the kids. I couldn't help but think, 'Well, obviously I'm on the crap teacher list,' which isn't fair because I'm pretty sure I'm one of the best teachers in the school. I've been meaning to email him or his secretary to set up another evaluation, when I have an actual lesson, and put on the show and all that kind of stuff.

"Here's my prediction. He'll probably set something up and then he won't show up. Either way, nothing will happen and he'll sign off something at the end of the year, just like he did last year. But let's change the subject."

"Okay," I responded, thankful to move on.

"There are people all over this school that I don't recognize and that I probably would see at the grocery store and not even know that we teach at the same school. I don't know a lot of the teachers' names, but nobody's really gone out of their way to be all that friendly with me in the first place. I remember somebody said to me earlier this year that a lot of the teachers don't talk to first-year teachers because they usually don't stick around. I do my best to be very friendly with everyone—the kids love me. I never really thought about it before but I think that teachers here don't wanna be bothered. If that's the way it is, then that's fine. But I guess it does make a certain environment. I don't leave my door open that much. I like quiet time for myself. I get so sick of those damned kids. I can't understand them half the time either. And so that's the only time that I'm going to get peace and quiet, when the students are not in my room. I eat lunch in here. I'm pretty much here from 8 a.m. until 3, then I walk to my car and go home."

"Sounds lonely," I said. "Don't you ever talk to the other teachers?"

Dustin thought for a minute. "I see them in committee meetings. Did you know I'm editing our accreditation report? I thought half of it was pretty good, but there were a few good chunks of it that were just total bullshit. There were other things on it that, on paper that's what we're doing. But in reality, we're not. Same with the School Improvement Plan. According to that, we have nine reading programs in place—do you know how many we really have? One! That stupid 15-minute reading thing. That's obviously what they're gonna pass off to the state, and that's fine, that's not my call, it's just a big game."

"Right," I said. "Do you think other people are doing things that you're not aware of?"

"I guess," Dustin replied. "But back to teaching. I've decided not to quit. I don't think I'll come back to DuBois if I can get a job somewhere else. We finished *King Lear* just this week because I'll have to split up the next one due to spring break. Which is not good, and I guess I could have planned for that, but oh well, I figure they can read over the break. They can't take home the books over break, but you can get Shakespeare anywhere if you really want to. Of course, none of them will read it. Too lazy. I got them to finally understand what the play's about. It's a miracle that they finally have a basic understanding. They don't like it, a lot of them didn't really read it—hell, a lot of them can't really read—but at least they finally have an understanding of it and they can actually accomplish something—like a test or a report. I'm kind of proud of myself. 'Cause man, they did terrible on the last test. Every single one failed. Nobody came close—the highest grade was a 50%. So obviously they just had no idea. They don't really care. Over half of them are failing my class and will fail it again next year.

"That's the thing I hate about this school. I hate that education is devalued in the Black culture. But, there's also this subversive sense that they'll squeak by. How did these kids get to 10th grade without being able to read? It's like I'm always caught in that trap. I'm sure it happens everywhere. I hate that. I just get angry at the choices they make. I actually said this to a few different classes, 'I'm tired. I'm tired of you guys expecting me to expect you to do nothing. I don't understand. Where are you getting this idea?' But it's there. And I think that it's because there's no continuity, there's really nobody who just says, No—you know what? Sorry." Dustin slammed his fist down on the desk for effect. "That's not how it's gonna be! You're not getting past me!" He grew quiet and smiled proudly.

"And I've changed the way that I've dealt with students individually. Last year I thought it was me with the problem. Now I say, 'No, *you* have a problem. I have my act together. This is not going to work and *you're* the one who is going to change.' And that works better. I'm demanding higher standards and holding students accountable."

I interrupted. "But, Dustin, you just told me you let students put their heads down on the desk if they don't want to participate."

"Right. I'm not talking about those kids. They're a lost cause. I'm talking about the rest of them. I think that's probably the change that I was looking for. I've been more direct in just saying, 'No, this is not how it's supposed to be.' They respond to that. I'm not a tough guy by nature. It's not who I am. But at the same time I want everybody to have a good chance to do well and I realize now that I'm the master in this classroom. It's sad because I hate people that act mean—I don't hate people—but I know what these kids need and they need structure and discipline.

"I read *Moby Dick* last summer, which is now my favorite book. I always wished I had read it. I finally did and I loved it. I didn't know I was going to love it that much. When I was reading it, everybody I know said, 'Oh, I read that in high school.' And after reading the book, I thought, why in the world would anybody teach that in high school? Maybe you could in a normal high school but these kids would be in over their heads from the first page. It's not really about whales at all, you know. It's about being a driven person, it's about having a goal and going after it, it's about focus and success. It's about humanity and everything about being alive. No high school kid—definitely no high school kid here—is going to get that."

"Some people say it's also about racism" I interjected.

"Some people say everything is about racism," Dustin responded. "It's like a Shakespeare play, it's like a James Joyce book. It has infinite depth. It's fantastic. Every chapter is almost like an allegory for a different human condition or experience, so it's almost like a book of philosophy, but told in this backdrop of hunting the whale. It's amazing! If I could get my students to appreciate something beautiful like that, it would rock their worlds. I don't think they have beauty, or amazing stories, or great writers in their worlds. You know what I mean?"

CHAPTER 5

The Black Leadership Experience: Living the Dream or Expelled to Excel?

Some of the chapters in this book may seem to describe a flat, Black/White dichotomy in the school. While this was the case in a broad sense, there was also a great deal of variation. This chapter relates four Black teachers' narratives around race and education and helps explain how they developed the beliefs that guided their actions.

PAUL ALPHONSE, GUIDANCE COUNSELOR

I'm from the West Coast, but I came down South to go to school. I finished my undergraduate degree in psychology and then moved on to counseling education, and that's where I received my master's. I'm a strong believer in education. I'm a product of an inner city, South Central Los Angeles, and I know the importance of education. To be blunt, where I come from you can pretty much gauge the success of people by looking at the importance of education within the household. Or, in some cases the level of importance individual kids place on education, despite their family's values. I may have been the only one in my class from my neighborhood to actually graduate from college. And I'm not just talking on my block, in my actual neighborhood. I've known of three people in my age range who have actually gone to college. I don't know if any of them graduated. I'm hoping that number has increased since I left, but I'm not optimistic.

So that environment has always stayed with me, has always stuck with me. I remember I had one teacher, her name was Ms. Nancy Brotherton, she was an English teacher—and for lack of a better word, she was a thorn in my side. She would not let me rest, no matter what. There could have been ten kids that were doing something wrong in that classroom. If I was in the vicinity, she would call my name and she would hound me, man. My freshman year I had her and she was on me all the time, but I also had her for my senior year in speech. That was an elective; you could either have English 4 or speech. I took her for speech, and I remember my mom came up to school, and it was a quarter grade, and I earned either an A or a B, but she gave me a grade lower. And she looked at my mom, I'll never forget, and she said, "He deserves a higher grade; I just won't give it to him because he's not trying. He just shows up. He's not working up to his potential. He just shows up, takes the test, and he's satisfied with that." And that angered me because at the time it didn't seem fair. I didn't realize until years later what she did. She actually tricked me because she knew my pride would not allow me to just sit and let that happen. And so from that day forward, I moved my seat to the front of the class voluntarily. I was always in the front of the class. I was ready, I was prepared because this was a turnaround for me. No one would take anything else from me academically.

And that's actually what started my spark—Ms. Brotherton—and I noticed that, as I became better with my grades people started to look toward me when it was time to make an answer, and that became addictive. So I actually enjoyed that, but as I moved through college, I realized that I may have something to offer. I began to feel I was obligated to give back. Because in my neighborhood, I was from a rough area. But Ms. Brotherton, and I didn't know this quite at the time, she was also from a very rough area. She was from Compton, and if you know anything about the layout of LA, South Central is very rough, but there are certain areas that even South Central can't compete with.

And so I've always had a passion for education. I did not originally go into education once I graduated because I had my degree, graduated with honors, and I was ready for the world. I didn't realize that I needed experience. I was book-smart but job-dumb. So when I came out I thought that I would get the dream job right away. I went for a job interview and I'm like hey, you know, I graduated with honors, I'm very open, flexible, I'm eager to learn. And the answer was, "Right. Those other 500 applicants said exactly the same thing." I had to work odd jobs here and there, but it taught me work ethic, and I actually appreciate that now. I worked for the state for about 5 or 6 years, in the Department of Family Services.

So, in a way, I was still moving toward school but I just was not in a classroom per se. Then one day I woke up and asked myself, is this what you really want to do, or do you really want to be in the school system? And I answered my question when I filled out the application. At that point I did have some relevant experience, so I was able to make the move.

I enjoy working at DuBois very much, and here you can see that you make a difference. You know, sometimes people say that jobs are rewarding, and they're not talking necessarily about money. It sounds like a bunch of bull until you're doing it. Unless you experience working in a place like this on a daily basis, you really don't understand what they're talking about. Five years ago I would have laughed at you myself if you told me being a teacher was rewarding. But you know, I've seen kids turned around, and not necessarily because of me; we have an awesome staff here. But I have been part of a few cases and that feeling to me is addictive because I remember where I came from, and I know without a shadow of a doubt that if education did not play a part in my life, let's just say I don't think I would be faring so well. Because when I go back home, I would say probably 85 to 90% of the people that I grew up with are either incarcerated, dead, or they're just struggling to get by day to day. I'm a product of that environment, so I know that if I did not have education, more than likely I probably would be in that situation. That's why I'm so charged up about letting the kids here know that it's not where you're from, it's where you're going. And we each get to decide whether we stand there in place or put one foot in front of the other and move forward. It's a very rewarding job. I enjoy it very much.

Now, let's be real, every day isn't a walk in the park. I remember we had this one young lady who was very belligerent. I want to laugh now because I just remember how she didn't want to go to class, she didn't want to participate when she went to class, and it came down to what I like to call "crunch time" for her. She was about a semester away from non-graduating, because she didn't do what she needed to do in terms of earning credits. And I think she realized at that point that she really, for lack of a better word, just, I'm gonna use one of their terms, screwed up. Tawanna was her name, Tawanna.

Tawanna was about to drop out, and we had a conference. It was me, another counselor, and Tawanna's father. Tawanna was really adamant, practically screaming, and she said look, you know, "I don't care what you say!" It was odd because she screamed at us with the parent right there. And it was a male parent, it wasn't a female. It wasn't the mom, it was the dad. That's rare here so it was out of the ordinary. And so she said, "I don't care, you know, what you do, what you say, I'm just not coming, period. You can punish me, you can do whatever!" The father said nothing. We tried to calm her down, which didn't seem to go very well, and then Tawanna and her father got up and left. We were so frustrated, it seemed like a lost cause.

Well, about 2 months later, we received a card, the other counselor and myself. We opened it up, and it was from Tawanna's father. I don't know what it said verbatim, but he said we had changed her attitude toward school by showing an interest in her, by caring. And that young lady graduated on time. And she, I mean she had to really make perfect marks, she probably made like all A's that last semester. I mean because she was really on the borderline but she pulled through. And that's just one—I've had several young men who were what the system would call delinquent; they've been in and out of the system and now they're on their way to graduate this year.

It's something special, when you've reached a kid. You can look in their eyes and there's a difference, there's a spark that wasn't there before. The funny thing about kids, and maybe adults too, is that they need validation. If they think that you can't understand where they're coming from or what they've been through, then it automatically sort of puts you in another category. But, you know, I can relate to a lot of their stories. Sometimes I won't share too much, but I do share some things with them. The one thing they all know—the kids, that is, most of my colleagues don't know this about me—is that I'm South Central. Though it's another part of the country, they know I'm one of them and I've seen a lot. Some of them may not know the city, but some of them know that I come from a rough neighborhood. I had every opportunity to make the wrong choice, make the wrong choices, and I don't lie to them. What happened in my case was I didn't make enough of the wrong choices, and I made enough of the right choices, you know. It's nothing about self-glory or anything like that, it's just basically telling them look, if I can make it, you can make it. And sometimes, that just makes a difference, just validating their concerns. A lot of them are scared. Scared to go home, scared of their future, scared of failure. And they've all been told they will fail from the day they got into school. I can see it in their eyes and I know that look, because I was scared, too. Those are the kids I work for—I work to give scared kids confidence.

MYRA WATKINS-GLENN, SOCIAL STUDIES TEACHER

My high school social studies teacher was very influential on me. She shared a lot of stories with us, with me, and we were a lot alike. I just pretty much followed in her footsteps. I really looked up to her and admired her, and I would always say I want to be just like her when I get older. She lives in my neighborhood where I grew up and everything so we still have a close relationship. It's because of her that I am where I am today.

I ended up going to college and majoring in chemistry, of all things, and then I changed my major to education and eventually found social studies. My mom wasn't too happy about that. But it was what I wanted to do. I earned the degree and then I ended up here. And I love my job, but at times it's rough. I have to admit that in some ways I feel I've grown as a teacher and at other times I'm not sure I'm cut out for it. For example, this year I'm teaching a lot of seniors and I noticed that I give more information to students who were doing well, like the honor students. I would give them more information about scholarships and I would talk to them more about that kind of stuff. I stopped doing that with students that weren't doing so well. I wasn't trying to put them down or anything, but I know which students are focused and I know which ones are not. I know what they all want to do, I know how accomplished some are versus these other students who aren't really as motivated. And maybe, just reflecting on myself, that's something I need to work on, trying to motivate them to push themselves a little harder.

I know teachers aren't supposed to doubt the abilities of the kids, but I do more and more. And sometimes it's hard because I see them come in here with the gold teeth and the glasses, shades, and I tell them I refuse to talk to any students with that. I refuse. They know they cannot come to my office and talk to Miss Watkins-Glenn with gold teeth in their mouth. They know that so they have to take it out, do whatever. I refuse to talk to them. I mean, I don't have any of my honor students that have that have a grill or dress like that. But the general education students are a different story.

I had a group of kids in here one day and most of them were in English honors. And then there were another group of students that came in and it seemed as if I had a closer relationship with those students that were doing well versus those that weren't as academically sound. I saw the way this little girl looked at me like, "Oh you like them better than you like us." And that's when I noticed. She didn't say anything, but I could tell in her body language. And she's thinking how come you don't talk to me like that.

They were trying to find something like some programs that may offer summer college tours, and so one of the kids asked if I would sponsor them to go on a college tour. And I said sure, let's get maybe ten students together. Then an honors student started going down the line of ten students and I said, no, he's not ready for that school. Or, no, she's not, oh yes, she's good, let's get her. And then this little girl in my general education class was right there when all of that was going on, and she kind of looked at me like, why didn't you call my name? That's how she looked at me—she was horrified. When I went home that day I thought about it, and I was conflicted. Maybe I should motivate them all. Maybe taking them on a college tour might motivate them all to go to college. I'm trying to be more open to all the students and treating them the same. But the other reason I was like that was because I read this article in the NEA magazine that we get every month and they were talking about teachers not being honest with their students and giving them false hope. False hope about going to college, and when I read that, I realize we've always told our students that they can go to college as though it's a birthright. But it isn't, especially for the Black kids. If you look at some of these kids' transcripts, you'll see they're D's and F's all over the place. They're really not going to be successful in college, even if they get in. I know some students may not do well in high school, but then they go to college and they're very successful. I know that, but that's the exception, not the rule. Anyway, after reading that article, I thought about it and asked my classes how many of them want to go to college—every last one raised their hand. But, honestly, not all of them are going to go to college.

My first year teaching I remember this little girl coming into my office. She came by after class to talk about her goals, her dreams. This girl really looked up to me. I asked her what she wanted to do. She was in 9th grade. And she said, I want to be a pediatrician. I had the computer open to her records and she had skipped 35 days of school before Christmas. And I think one thing is that a lot of our students now are, I think, the ones that are graduating, are going to be maybe the first ones in their family to get a high school diploma. The ones who don't graduate, don't truly realize what they are doing. They don't really understand. They just take today for today and that's it. They don't look toward their future. And part of me thinks that me being here at DuBois is so important because I can really relate to them and I'm young and relatively close to their age and so they see, oh, Miss Watkins-Glenn can go to college and be successful, I can do that, too.

And I tell them about when I went to college my freshman year I almost got kicked out of school. I was on academic probation after my freshman year. I tell them about how I got the letter in the mail. I intercepted the letter. And it said you have a 1.5 GPA. You'll be on academic probation for the next semester and you have to bring it up to a 2.0 GPA. It wasn't that low, but something like that, one point something. I told them when I received that letter in the mail I was stunned, because I was an A/B student in high school. College was my first time away from home.

It's freedom. And I tell them that story and, you know, just to show them that you can do it, too, you know. And so after that I didn't play any more because I could not get kicked out of college, you know. That was just going to be the biggest disappointment. And then I'm the first college graduate in my family because my family is from Jamaica. And then I'm the first-generation American. So, you know, I just try to give the stories about where my family comes from, and what my family went through to be here and, you know, the sacrifices that my parents have made.

And then I also tell them that you all don't realize it, but being from this country, even though being in America they may be poor, but to other third-world countries, people in those countries, they're rich. They're rich. Rich. Full of opportunity. They can do whatever they want to do. They have free education. You know, I try to explain that to them. Some of them understand, but most of them don't understand where I'm coming from. I just went to Jamaica maybe about a month ago and I brought back pictures and when I came back I went and showed some of the students some of my pictures. And we went to one of the schools and I just showed them pictures of the kids. And, you know, they actually saw like some of the poverty, and I think that some of them really understood like, wow, they're really poor. You know, they're just walking around with no shoes on. Just old clothes and, you know, so I, you know, try to teach them that, but I don't think that a lot of them understand where I'm coming from.

Another thing that I'm trying to make sense of at the school is how racial and ethnic and cultural dynamics play out in the school. It seems to me people ignore these differences, except on rare occasions usually having to do with food or holidays. These things cause problems, not in and of themselves, but because we don't talk about difference around here. Difference scares people and so they don't talk about it. Nothing is ever said about it. Nothing is said about race, about gender, about sexuality, nothing about culture or ethnicity. I mean a lot of what goes on here is part of their culture and ethnicity but they see those as synonymous with race. These kids run around and out of here because that's all that they know. They don't know any better.

So, I mean, even with slang that they use. They think I'm down, but I wasn't raised that way. My mother would slap me in my mouth for coming home speaking slang the way these kids do. We moved here when I was 10, and being raised here in America around African American children, I was teased for the way that I speak. You know, they would tell me, "You talk like a White girl." I didn't really understand because my parents have an accent and a lot of my parents' friends were also from the Caribbean, so we all pretty much spoke the same. I don't have an accent like my parents do—they kidded with me about my U.S. accent. So, I just really didn't understand that at the time. Like how do Black people talk versus White people talk.

But then I went to a historically Black college, and then I learned a lot about African Americans and just the culture here and how different it is. Now I understand why they would say I talk like a White girl. I still get that to this day—in fact, there's an administrator, a Black man, who thinks it's funny to make fun of my accent and he's done it in faculty meetings—but in my mind I just speak standard English, proper English. That's just how I was raised to speak.

My experience with language makes me then wonder, again, is these kids' culture being respected and being used as something to build on when they're being taught in the classrooms, or are people just kind of like blasting them for speaking poorly, for dressing poorly, for being stupid in a school that doesn't honor their culture? That's all that they know, they don't know any different and they're told that what they know isn't correct.

DᴇSHAWN MOONEY, ENGLISH TEACHER

I think we could change the level of expectation, and once you do that, you make them reach a little bit more, I think that could bring up some scores. Unfortunately, a lot of African Americans buy into the "if I can just get by, that's good enough." And then there's—I know, like, for me being a male—African American male, you've got a reputation to protect. You know, you don't want to be a nerd. You don't want to be the one that's always going to class and getting the A's and stuff. You don't want to stick out in that way. It isn't cool. If you go that way you'll get cracked on, you'll get clowned and everything like that. And also you'll be considered White, and that's in the negative sense. One of the worst things you can call someone is a White boy, a cracker they say here. And that happens from your friends and sometimes from family members, you know. And all that mixed in with the culture that we have, we don't really promote education a lot, you know. We promote basketball. We promote sports, we promote other types of lifestyles instead of going to college. Black people get pissed off when a White person points that out, but I think it's true. And I think that expectation, that success looks like Kobe Bryant or a ghetto superstar like Master P, plays a huge role in it, you know. As long as you can just get by with a hustle, knowing what you know without putting in a lot of effort, that's good enough. It's even admired.

It's such a cliché but I think you need more positive role models. I try not to just isolate myself up in the room, you know, and try to go out and talk to a lot of the kids. Just social stuff. I want them to see a successful educated Black man. I work with a lot of the football players and basketball players and try to motivate them. It's the theory that if you have a lot of talent, and if you have academics on top of that, you can pretty much write a ticket to wherever you want to go in life. And you try to make them see the education and the business side of it instead of just straight athleticism.

And let's be real, I'm a nerd to them—I'm a teacher! Some of them might look at me as a failure, not a success. But I just try to let them see the positive influence. I'm respected and I'm respectful, I want them to see that. I know myself and some of the other African American teachers like Mr. Trappet, Mr. Johnson, and Steve Diggs try to get out there and circulate. We talk about our responsibility to be role models. You know, we try to let them see that you can be successful by getting your education. Because the way the world's moving now, you're going to need a college degree to get a job, not just a high school diploma, and if they don't have that, then they're going to be stuck.

So being in the halls is fine, but you have to connect to African American students in the classroom, that's where it really matters. And so my objective then is to sell them on this stuff. Then I can teach them whatever I want. As long as you can sell them, on myself, on what I'm teaching, anything I can do to get them, then I can teach them whatever I want. It's about engagement. And I think that's the thing that a lot of teachers don't do because it's an 8:00 to 3:00 effort. If you make it interesting and try to liven it up a little bit without losing the message, I think that'll help out a lot.

I don't know if it's only a race issue, it's a race-plus issue. What I mean by that is that race gives me a place to start. They trust me initially because of that but there's more, there's age, gender, all kinds of things. We have to use all of those things, and more, to make a connection with a kid. It's a fine line; you want to keep the teacher–student relationship professional. You don't want to cross over and be friends, but I think a lot of teachers are so afraid of crossing that line that they don't reach out and try to connect. Or some feel they don't get paid to do that, you know, to take an interest in a kid's life. But that's sad, because when you're teaching them, you're a part of their life. I see them 6 hours a day, and I really need to be a useful, a positive part of this person's life.

Honestly, we have a lot of older teachers, and I don't know if they're willing to make that connection.

Engagement is really scary for a lot of people, but it's just good teaching. I mean, you learn their life story, which is unique. Everyone is unique. And then you get to learn how to deal with that particular kid. I know it isn't in the curriculum, but I do this by not talking about English all the time. I set aside time for us to discuss other things. We talk about anything that's not dealing with words. That way, you end up learning a lot about them. For me, after I hear them talk a bit I take an interest in them as people and not just as students. You just listen. And after a while they tend to open up a little bit. I ask them how their other studies are going, what they are doing outside of school, that kind of stuff. One of the questions I work toward is, and they sometimes think it's mean, is, what are you doing with your life? And then, they'll say something and I respond with another question—is it positive?

PAUL REGIS, SCIENCE TEACHER

Look, to tell you the truth, some of the worst stuff I've seen in this school isn't White on Black racism, it's Black on Black. Brothers hatin' on brothers and sisters hatin' on sisters. Let me give you a few examples. First off, I know you're not from the South so you probably don't know this term, but down here we got porch niggers and field niggers. Ever heard of that? Well, porch niggers are the folk that made the decision to do the White man's bidding. They chose to play the game of being the submissive brother—or sister—and just play the White man's game. These are the Black folk who are acting White to get ahead. They forget who they are, they forget about their neighborhoods, and they forget about Black culture because they see that if they are the good, obedient slave, they can get ahead in life. We have a lot of those in the schools. They dress like White folk, they talk like them, and they are often the token Black on those committees. They toe the party line. It's never about race with them, it's always about something else. They're sellouts, far as I'm concerned.

Field niggers is like me. I work in the sun. I toil. I carry a heavy load but it makes me strong. I may have less than the porch nigger, but I have my dignity. I have pride. This is a real split in the Black educational community. There are those who choose the porch and those who choose the field. A few people can go back and forth, but that's only a few. Usually, people who try to do that eventually end up on one side or the other. You can't have it both ways and be real.

Here's an example, the principal here is on the porch. He doesn't care about his people, doesn't care about the kids. Hell, he doesn't know most of their names. What he cares about is pleasing the White people at the district office. How do you do that? By closing the achievement gap, by increasing student achievement and earning a higher letter grade for the school, right? Well, here's how we did that last year. The principal rounded up a bunch of kids who are in the lowest level on the things that the state test assesses. You know, the kids who can't read, can't do math—the lowest we have in terms of academic performance. He rounded them up in the library, and I know because I was there. Anyway, he put these kids at all these tables. All the faces were Black, and that kills me. He put these kids at the table and gave them a serious fire-and-brimstone sermon. I mean, he laid it on thick, telling them that they weren't going to amount to anything and that it was a waste of time for them to be in school. They should be at home helping their families, working, or getting a GED. He put Voluntary Withdrawal Forms in front of each of them and told them they had to sign them. It was awful. He told them to sign the forms and then bring them to his office later in the day. He said he wanted them that day. Guess what day that was? It was Monday the week before we started our head count for the state test. It meant that they wouldn't be counted in our numbers for the school's grade. I mean, to please the White folk, to please the public I guess, he kicked those kids on the street with no education. That's a damned shame to do to anyone, but to be a Black man and do it to a bunch of Black kids is criminal.

So, yeah, there is racism at DuBois. There always has been and always will be, but it's not just the White people doing bad things to the Black people. We don't even look out for our own. We segregate within our own community and beat up on each other. I love my people, I love my Black brothers and sisters, but we're not only victims—we are perpetrators sometimes, too.

GOOD TEACHERS ARE MORE THAN GOOD TEACHERS

The narratives in this chapter underscore the notion that good teaching is not only about technique and knowledge in the classroom, but about connecting to communities and people. This connection impacts a single student, to be sure, but it also has the potential to impact generations of students and families. This suggests a collateral benefit of instruction that helps engage students and show them that their work in schools is connected to the rest of their lives. In the previous chapter, we heard Dustin craft a narrative of hate, privilege, and ignorance. His teaching and beliefs about his students were much like a weapon aimed at the destruction of student self-esteem. Alternately, the narratives in this chapter suggest a counternarrative of hope, emancipation, solidarity, and culturally relevant education as a key to personal and professional growth.

CHAPTER 6

That Program Ain't Never Done a Thing for Black Kids . . . or Has It?

As a beginning teacher, I was given low-level classes. Kids that need remedial help. They were predominantly black. As I gained years there, I started getting honors classes. They were overwhelmingly white. Right now I have one black child in my honors class, out of twenty-seven.

—Teacher Peter Soderstrom, quoted in Studs Terkel's
*Race: How Blacks and Whites Think and Feel
About the American Obsession* (1992, p. 192)

I've studied school reform and programming, but I had never been close to an International Baccalaureate (IB) program before I visited DuBois. I knew a bit about the basics of IB but that was it. The first time I walked into the school's main office, I picked up a flyer about the program and made a note to ask about it in upcoming interviews. As it happened, my interviewee that morning was Steven, a White assistant principal, who told me IB was "something like AP. Basically, it's an honors program for smart kids." I didn't give it much more thought until the following afternoon when I interviewed a Black language arts teacher named Sidney Moncleur. He explained the program like this: "You ever heard of FUBU? It's a brand of clothes for kids. It stands for 'For Us, By Us' and the *us* is Black folk. It's our own brand of clothes. That's how the IB program is, but in reverse—it's For *Them*, By *Them*—and I mean White folk. That program ain't never done a thing for Black kids." In the margins of my notes from Sidney's interview I wrote: "second-generation segregation?"

Second-generation segregation is a term used to explain how school segregation continues in a post-*Brown v. Board* era, as something happening systematically *within* schools. It refers to "forms of racial segregation that are a result of school practices such as tracking, ability grouping, and the misplacement of students in special education classes" (Spring,

2006, p. 83). In U.S. public schools, this often means that students of color are placed in remedial or special education courses, while White students represent a majority of those placed in honors courses (Patton, 1998; Perry, Steele, & Hilliard, 2003; Valles, 1998; Zhang & Katsiyannis, 2002). Second-generation segregation is a largely silent, but powerful and systematic form of institutional racism in American education. Singleton and Linton (2006) argue that AP programs in particular are often overt manifestations of this form of racism, which sends very clear messages to *all* students.

> When White students enter an advanced placement classroom and see few if any students of color, they are unconsciously indoctrinated into White intellectual supremacy. These notions are typically unchallenged by educators, even as students of color learn about these classes, made up of mostly White students, and labeled as the "smart," "honors," "gifted," "advanced," "GATE," or "best" class. Not seeing others who look like them in these classes, the students of color will see themselves as being incapable of performing at equally high levels and feel unwanted in such classes or unworthy of taking them. Furthermore, because these classes are often taught by the more seasoned and respected teachers—the teachers who express passion for their work—the students of color are essentially taught by the system that they are worth less than White students. (pp. 43–44)

Put differently, in second-generation segregation programs, White students learn of their privilege and superiority through a hidden curriculum, while students of color learn an inverse lesson—they are inferior, academically and perhaps socially. And since these tracks, programs, and labels tend to stay with students throughout their school days, the messages are reinforced over and over, from student to student and from generation to generation (Patton, 1998).

A quick glance through the IB website (http://www.ibo.org/) left me with the impression that while it had a global focus, the program was indeed very much like many honors-type programs I had studied (Brooks, 2006a, 2006c; Brooks, Scribner, & Eferakorho, 2004). I was scheduled to observe a class in the IB program a few days later and I had an interview with the program coordinator in just a week, so I knew I would learn more in short order.

On the day I observed IB teacher Brenda Marsden's Theory of Knowledge (TOK) course, pairs of students were delivering presentations. I was a little put off when I found this out, because while I always enjoy and learn a great deal by viewing student work, I had hoped to watch a more naturalistic session, one that was "typical." What I saw during that 50-minute period astounded me. The student presentations were extremely high-level—much more advanced than I asked of my graduate students at the university. They had chosen focus topics, such as poverty, and investigated them from multiple disciplinary perspectives. The poverty presentation included information from sociological, anthropological, and political science research, and entailed an analysis and critique of various claims made in articles, books, census reports, and popular media, and by local policymakers and politicians. The presentation also included a detailed look at poverty in the local community and suggestions for service-learning projects the students could undertake to make a positive influence. Moreover, these were not idle suggestions; the students showed how they could create metrics to adjudge the effectiveness of each strategy, and announced that they soon would be choosing one of these options for their service-learning project. The project would be designed over the following semester, implemented that summer, and evaluated over the following year. A presentation on sustainable agriculture followed poverty, while another was concerned with watershed conservation. A final presentation explored the issue of hunger. To say I was impressed by the quality of the work and the students' ability to speak about these topics as experts is an understatement—I was astonished by this display of intellectual talent and oratory skill. In fact, I was so taken aback that I nearly forgot to write down an important detail that was immediately relevant to my study: of the eight students who presented, five were Black.

A few days later I interviewed the IB program coordinator, Natasha Frye. We met in her office suite, a weary cluster of small rooms tucked out of sight in the lower side of DuBois's eastern wing. While the walls and doors showed their age, the rooms themselves were impeccably clean and in strict order. Files and boxes labeled with various clear markings were stacked neatly in rows, and the surfaces of counters, desks, and tables were clear, save for a few papers teachers were grading as they sipped coffee. The space seemed serene compared with the hustle and bustle of DuBois's noisy hallways. "Nat" welcomed me, and after we exchanged pleasantries she asked me to sit in an empty chair near her desk. We turned to regard the computer, which showed an excerpt from the DuBois School Improvement Plan. She gave me a few minutes to read as she finished up a few things in preparation for our interview.

> The international baccalaureate program is a magnet offering opened in 1996, which draws academically motivated students from the entire school district. The students in IB represent multiple ethnic, economic, and racial backgrounds. DuBois's 358 IB students make up approximately 27% of the total population of the school.

The curriculum for grades 9 and 10 consists of a pre-IB foundational structure designed to provide the student with sufficient academic, analytic, theoretical, and practical skill to perform at an international level. The 11th- and 12th-grade curriculum consists of comprehensive and rigorous formal curriculum sanctioned by the IB Curriculum and Assessment Centre in Cardiff, Wales. Each course of study concludes with an internationally standardized examination. The general objectives of the IB are to provide students with a balanced education, to facilitate geographic and cultural mobility, and to promote international understanding through a shared academic experience.

In order to receive the international baccalaureate diploma, students must complete the curriculum as prescribed by the International Baccalaureate Organization (IBO). Course work for the junior and senior years requires instruction in English (Language A), a secondary language, experimental science, social studies, mathematics, and a sixth subject. Sixth-subject offerings at DuBois include an additional language or science, art, psychology, and theatre. Students must score successfully on IB exams in all six of these subjects. A theory of knowledge course must be successfully completed as well. In addition, between 10th and 12th grades students must participate in at least 200 documented hours of extracurricular creativity, action, and service as well as write and present a supervised extended essay of at least 4,000 words.

When I finished and looked up at her, Nat was beaming, and proceeded to tell me some of the program's accomplishments.

"Just last year, we had three National Merit finalists, five National Achievement commendations, and 100% of our students gained admission to a college or university. We sent a kid to Harvard and another to Yale. Our 53 seniors earned a total of 54 scholarships, and 88% of our students earned the IB diploma—and that's quite a feat!" She had all these numbers memorized.

I scribbled some notes in my notebook. "Very impressive," I replied, looking down rather than at her. She waited for me to stop writing and raise my eyes, then continued.

"What's more," Nat said, "you might be interested to know that we make the district about $350,000 a year."

Nat explained: "We make whatever the FTE value is. For every IB test a kid passes, they bring an additional quarter of an FTE, which is around $1,000. And, then, my seniors, if they get a diploma, they bring in an additional, I believe, oh . . . 30% of an FTE. So, every test we pass is worth several hundred dollars to us; the teachers get a small cut for each student who passes the exam in their area. It isn't much, but it adds up and for some teachers it can mean a few thousand extra—that's a lot for a teacher. You might say we have a built-in incentive pay program.

"Last year IB kids brought in $350,000 to the district, and $250,000 of that goes to this school, which is how we have stuff that other teachers and programs don't. That money is *supposed* to *all* go back into the program." I noticed that Nat stressed the words *supposed* and *all*.

"It's supposed to go back? Do you mean that it doesn't actually come back to the program?" I asked.

"Right, it doesn't. Here's how it works: The district takes about 33% off the top and gives us, well, they always give us $250,000. Sometimes it's a little more or less than 33% but it's not a big deal. That's all legitimate. So, I supposedly have a budget of $250,000 a year for the program. I run this office on about $75,000. We buy all of our books from that fund. I get all the supplies for every IB teacher and anybody else who teaches my kids, since we can't cover every single course ourselves. They get supplies and access to everything we have, which means their departments don't have to do it. This is what the faculty doesn't understand. We essentially take care of 27% of the kids at this school and a whole bunch of teachers without touching the school's operating budget, other than whatever pays our salaries."

"So the IB program is self-sustaining," I responded.

"And then some. But there's a problem." Nat let out a sigh and rocked back in her chair.

"Oh," I asked, "what problem? It sounds like a pretty good set-up."

Nat gave me a once-over, sizing me up as she decided how much to tell me. After a long pause, she deadpanned, "The problem is the principal."

"How do you mean?"

"He takes our money and uses it for other things in line with his agenda that have nothing to do with IB. Dr. Ferguson actually announced at a meeting the other day that he has paid salaries out of IB and AP funds. That's not permissible, and it might even be illegal. Those funds are only supposed to be used to support the IB program. I now know he paid John Cabrini's salary one year, and he's a guidance counselor who has nothing to do with IB. Doc [the principal] is ultimately responsible for how the money's used; he has an oversight role—but after his first year at DuBois he discovered a loophole. The school operating budget and the IB budget are kept separate. We're a magnet program, and in some ways our money works kind of like a grant. It's not included in the general operating budget. Technically, he is in charge of the IB budget because it is a school-level program, but there's no follow-through or accountability and he does what he pleases with it. They audit him for the school budget but they don't audit ours." Nat's voice trailed off as she finished that last sentence and she turned toward her desk and shuffled some papers. She continued to speak over her shoulder. "It's a more modest budget, but he does it with the AP funds, too."

"Isn't there someone you can speak with about this at the district?" I asked.

"Theoretically, yes; practically, no. They won't do anything."

"Why not?" I wondered. "It seems to me that if there's evidence of that kind of misappropriation of funds, then surely someone would . . . "

Nat interrupted me. "It's race, Jeff—no one will do anything because he's Black. They all know what he's doing but they won't do anything about it. He has accused people at the district of being racist in the past. They're terrified. He's a few years away from retirement and they think, oh, we'll just look the other way for a few years."

I wasn't sure how to respond to that, so I remained silent, scribbling away in my notepad.

Nat raised her voice, "Oh, it's race! Race! Oh, my God, and I don't have a problem saying it even though there's no school-wide dialogue around it at all here. There should be, but it's like . . . "

This time I interrupted Nat. "It's the elephant in the schoolhouse."

"Huh?"

"Race is the elephant in the schoolhouse. A friend of mine, Joan Wynne (2003), wrote a chapter in a book where she made that argument. No one will talk about it, but it has tremendous influence on what happens in schools. You can't see, move, or listen around it, but everyone acts as though the elephant, as if race, isn't really there."

"Bingo," exclaimed Nat. "Your friend described this school perfectly."

I fidgeted for a second, considering my next interview prompt. "Now, I hope you'll be okay with this question, but I have to ask one that might be uncomfortable related to race."

"Shoot," Nat exclaimed. "Now this is getting interesting. I doubt, though, that you'll make me uncomfortable. I was a civil rights activist in Mississippi in my younger years. I helped integrate a school system and got death threats for leading a committee that created a multicultural curriculum." There was a gleam in her hazel eyes again.

"Okay," I responded. "Maybe it's just me who's uncomfortable. Anyway, do you think the IB program is one of those programs that perpetuates racism?"

Nat's grin melted into a frown. "Jeff, I don't really understand your question."

I nervously stammered, "Well, in another interview someone told me that the IB program has never done anything for Black kids. You know, research suggests that in schools like this Black students, especially Black males, are referred into special education while the White students are in the honors and gifted programs like IB. It's called second-generation segregation and it's a form of institutional racism."

Visibly perturbed, Nat didn't say anything. Instead, she swiveled back around in her chair and fished out a piece of paper. She handed it to me. "Look at this, Jeff—the IB program is 41% African American students." I took the paper and examined it (see Table 6.1).

I was surprised to see these demographics, which were completely out of line with my assumptions and what other people had said. "This is really strange. I spoke to a teacher a few days ago who said that IB never did anything for Black kids. What could he have meant?"

Nat let out a sigh and asked me, "Didn't you go to T.O.K. [Theory of Knowledge] a few days ago—what did the students look like?"

"Well, I guess you're right. A little less than half the students were Black," I mumbled.

"Right, they were Black. And mind you, the 'Other' in that table I just handed you also includes African students. Not African American, but recent immigrants. And my teaching faculty is diverse too, for that matter: Harvey Crumpton, Molly Nuster, Wanda Simpson, Shawana Mayfield, Sara Rison, and Mary Marshall—all Black. Juana Gutierrez is Mexican. Alma Little is mixed, you know, mixed race, or however you categorize it. Mr. Dawson, Michael Dawson, is Black. It wasn't intentional, but we actually mirror the IB population pretty well. Now guess what—that's about seven more Black teachers than any other IB program in the state, I can tell ya. I don't know this for sure, but I imagine we are one of the more diverse programs in the country, maybe in the world. Because nationally, there are almost no Black people teaching in IB, and there are no Black kids in IB in most other programs. We go to IB conferences all the time and the most I've ever noted was that one school said they had 10%. Most of them are in the 2 to 4% range, and the people at Stilldon High, where the coordinator is a friend of mine, and she said she's never had a Black male get the diploma, *never*—and they are 4 years older than we are."

"So," I asked. "Really, this IB program is something of an anomaly. Those kinds of numbers are extremely uncommon, as far as I know from the research on other honors-type programs."

"Here's the best part," whispered Nat, as she leaned a little closer. "Dr. Ferguson knows all of that. I shared those emails. I sent emails to every coordinator in the state and said give me feedback on your African American

Table 6.1. International Baccalaureate Enrollment by Race and Gender

	9th			10th			11th			12th			Grand Total
	Male	*Female*	*Total*	*Male*	*Female*	*Total*	*Male*	*Female*	*Total*	*Male*	*Female*	*Total*	
Caucasian	13	25	38	18	17	35	13	22	35	19	16	35	143 (40%)
African American	16	43	59	17	13	30	10	23	33	7	18	25	147 (41%)
Asian	5	10	15	5	10	15	3	8	11	5	3	8	49 (14%)
Hispanic	3	0	3	0	1	1	1	3	4	0	0	0	8 (2%)
Other	4	3	7	0	0	0	1	1	2	1	1	2	11 (4%)
Grand Total	41	81	122	40	41	81	28	57	85	32	38	70	358

population. How many Black kids? How many girls? How many boys? Black girls do great in this program, but they don't have many anywhere. They have—well, we have always had 25 to 35% in our program. This year it's even a little bit higher."

"Okay." I nodded, listening intently.

Nat reached over and took a long sip of coffee, then continued. "And the White kids. If you're talking about skin color, they're White, but a lot of the White kids are Bulgarians and Danes and whatever else. We have 35 different countries represented in our program, but if you're going to look just at race, if you're only going to look at people and ignore their ethnicity or culture, we're about even . . . White and Black. We're much more multicultural than we are racially diverse. I show all this to Dr. Ferguson and the entire school staff every year. I have seven, eight Black teachers in this program. I have Hispanic people teaching, you know. He doesn't care, and people keep saying we're a program for White kids. To Doc it's a program for White kids taught by White teachers. End of story. Data be damned!" There was an air of finality about the way she ended that sentence, but after a moment her brow started to wrinkle. Something still wasn't sitting well with Nat.

"Well . . . " she began again. "It's about class, too. Dr. Ferguson is an elitist Black person. He's middle class, or upper middle class. He lives in one of those posh neighborhoods north of town where a lot of our more affluent students live. He drives a BMW. And what's more, he really looks down his nose at the Black IB teachers. Somehow he thinks of them as sell-outs." She paused.

"That's interesting," I started. "Have you ever heard of John Ogbu?"

"Oh I certainly have," said Nat.

"Well, I don't know what you've read, but what you are talking about makes me think of some work he did with Signithia Fordham (see Fordham, 1996; Fordham & Ogbu, 1986; Ogbu, 1978) about Black kids acting White. The basic gist of it was that Black kids who are successful in school are ostracized by their peers and branded a sell-out, like you were saying."

"Mm, hm," she hummed.

I kept going. "Based on what you say, it makes me wonder if that isn't how Dr. Ferguson sees the Black teachers in the IB program. Maybe he thinks they are selling out and acting White by teaching in a program that in his mind is for White people, even if most of the students in there are actually Black."

"I think that's probably correct. And the irony of it is that he does the same thing! He's always talking about how this is a Black neighborhood school, and that because I'm not Black and don't live in their neighborhood I can never understand the *real* DuBois students. He's suggested to

me on several occasions and he even said it in a faculty meeting last spring
to the entire school—that White teachers don't understand the Black kids
and they never will. But *he* lives on the north side of town in a predominantly White neighborhood. I've never even heard of him setting foot in
the neighborhoods he's talking about. He doesn't go to Fallson Ridge or
Hepton Commons where the two biggest gangs in the school operate. I
was there last week. I have former students who live there and keep me in
the loop about what's happening there. I know the IB kids' parents who
live there. It's the height of hypocrisy for Doc to say that to me and get in
a BMW for a drive to West Egg" (reference to a privileged neighborhood
in F. Scott Fitzgerald's novel *The Great Gatsby*). Nat said, "Now, there's
another thing that puzzles me about his hatred for the IB program. We're
the only reason the school is still open."

"What do you mean, Nat?"

With a wave of her hand, Nat produced another report (see Table 6.2).
"Take a look at this."

Table 6.2. Performance of IB and General Education Students on State
Examinations

	IB	Core	Total
Verbal Component			
No. of Students	358	1093	1451
No. Passing	315	295	610
Passing Rate	88%	27%	42%
Math Component			
No. of Students	358	1093	1451
No. Passing	357	284	641
Passing Rate	99%	26%	44%

I studied the table for a moment. The numbers were so striking . . .
so awful, that they hardly seemed real. "Let me get this straight," I said.
"Does this mean that only 26 or 27% of the general education students in
the school pass the verbal and math portions of the state test?"

"That's right," she said. "And that 26% *includes* the AP program. The
numbers for IB prevent the school from being shut down and reconsti-
tuted. According to the state's policies, the school would have what they
call a Triple F—failing 3 years in a row. All the teachers and administrators
are let go in that situation, and the school would reopen from scratch with

a new staff. That would happen to DuBois without IB. I was at the magnet meeting a few weeks ago, where we all share this stuff and everybody sees my data. The district superintendent was there, too. Another AP coordinator said to me, 'Nat, tell me what they're doing in the regular classes there. How the hell can you all have a 99% passing rate in math and have a 44 for the school? How can that be true?' I said, I don't know. I just run the IB classes. I don't know how to tell you what's going on. I have opinions. I have perceptions. For example, our attrition rate is really high. We lose about a third of our teachers every year here."

"Right," I responded. "That's unfortunately common at schools like DuBois."

"Sure," Nat acknowledged. "But to be honest, I *don't* know what's going on in a lot of those classes, largely because we never discuss any of the data the way we should. It gets buried, both inside the school and at the district level. The reason the district and Doc don't want the data desegregated is quite clear, and if you notice, you never see it in the news like this when the state announces results. I mean when you look at the way they present it you say, 'Okay, 44% of the kids passed reading at DuBois,' or whatever the number is."

"Lies, damned lies, and statistics," I responded.

"What?" said Nat, lost in thought.

"Something Disraeli once said," I offered. "Never mind. But I know what you mean about the ways people can mess around with data to give the message they want to give."

"Right," Nat said. I could tell she was beginning to tire of the interview. "If they'd spend that much time and energy addressing the problem, it would be fixed. But here's the thing. I don't really know why we are treated the way we are treated. From my perspective, the IB program is a national, maybe even international model of diversity and excellence. We're damned good and our students score very high on the state's tests. We send kids off to college—many who wouldn't normally go to college and we often send them on a free ride. We send kids to Harvard, to Yale, to Princeton. Black kids and White kids alike. I'm baffled and a little frustrated that the principal and some other teachers, too, view us as a bunch of Whitey Teachers educating our Whitey Kids. I've heard that exact phrase, by the way. It's complicated. I think it's mostly race, but it's all mixed up with issues of class, of economics, of society as a whole, but the people who need an enlightened perspective simply don't have one. We ought to be having a school-wide dialogue about issues of race at DuBois, but I can't raise them because I'm White, and other people can't raise them because they're Black. That's the norm here—the battle lines are drawn by race and you'd better not engage the enemy or you lose by instigation. So here I am, with all this data that could open a meaningful conversation and debunk some of the racial mythology of the place, but no one is interested. These are hard facts I'm sharing with you that ought to inform what we do in this school, but it feels like all I do sometimes is provide filler for reports."

"Let's call it a day, Nat," I suggested. "I'll get in touch with you to schedule a follow-up interview before too long if that's all right. Thanks for your time."

"All right," she mumbled, lost in thought. "It's nice to be able to talk about all this but it also gets me steamed up."

A bell rings as I leave the IB office and suddenly students fill the hallway. It's as though the dike that held them back has burst. I step to the side and watch the stream of students pass by. They are all shades of Brown and White—mostly Brown. A familiar in-the-halls-of-high-school jocularity and banter fills the air and the space between students. They make plans to meet later on the fly, they tease one another about clothes and hairstyles. Someone drops a book, and curiously leaves it there. Some students sprint down the halls trying to avoid being tardy, or hurriedly get out to the parking lot, a major social hub of the school. Others lazily saunter toward their destinations, in no particular rush. Many students produce cell phones from their pockets and sneak illicit glances at text messages—cell phones are banned and confiscated if students are caught using them during the normal school day. Just as suddenly as they appeared, the throng of students thins and then dries to a trickle. A few stragglers dart down the hallway and disappear through rust-rimmed blue metal doors. I dig through my bag and find the schedule. I should be in Harvey Crompton's room.

Harvey is the only graduate of DuBois who teaches at the school. He is an award-winning IB mathematics instructor and has won accolades as an outstanding early-career teacher, and for his students' outstanding performance on IB examinations. We open the interview by discussing his background. When Harvey was in IB as a student, he was inspired to become a math teacher, and he started the work as a senior. His capstone service-learning project was to create a tutoring program staffed by IB students. The program served non-IB students, and in particular it ended up helping many of the school's football and basketball players. Each team was a perennial contender for the state championship in their sport, but were occasionally undone by academic ineligibility.

Harvey explained, "Basically, my best friend and I had to do something for our service project for IB, so what we did was to take IB students, including ourselves, and matched them up with other students around DuBois to help them get tutoring. We tutored in everything from study and test-taking skills for the state exam to straight math, science, foreign language—any subject that they needed. None of us were experts but all of us could help. We did one-on-one sessions, and coordinated it so we could match up tutors and students based on their strengths and weaknesses. Here's an example. Some of the first guys we helped were a couple of football players who needed to get a certain score to get a certain scholarship. And one of the kids just, like, could not stand math . . . hated math . . . wanted nothing to do with math. We were trying to help him, and it just would not stick. So what I decided to do was . . . go to the bank. And I got as much possible change and dollars and stuff and broke it down to him with money, and it stuck—it just clicked. And right then he was like, 'You took this and you made it so simple.' Right then I thought, 'This feels pretty good. I'm good at this.' That guy went on to get his $200,000 scholarship to wherever he played . . . I can't even remember where it was. I saw him later and he was in this nice Escalade. He was really cool, and said, 'Thank you for helping me.' I was like, 'Oh you're welcome. Can I get a kickback?' We both laughed about that. Of course I wasn't serious. But anyway, it reminded me that my mom would always say, 'To whom much is given, much is expected.' I'm blessed with some ability in math and I'm blessed to be able to teach. It just always felt natural for me to be a teacher. You know, just helping people succeed and getting letters and emails from former students, and them coming back to visit you. Wow. It's just the greatest reward. I know it sounds all cheesy but it really is the greatest thing that I've experienced as a teacher. The thing that's a real challenge for me is *school*, rather than *teaching*."

"How do you mean?" I puzzled.

"Well, I mean all the rules. Like, you have to dress this way and you have to do this and that."

Pause. "Hm. I didn't think DuBois had a dress code for teachers."

"I guess we don't, but there are . . . I guess, some unwritten rules," Harvey laughed.

"Rules?"

"Sure. Like, Doc has this 'rule' [Harvey made little quotation marks in the air] that male teachers should wear a coat and tie to work." I looked Harvey over from head to toe: jeans, checkerboard skater-style shoes, and a red baggy sweater.

"What happened to that rule?" I asked. We both laughed.

"Well, Doc gave me a speech about how Black men in a Black school need to be role models. We need to show kids that we clean up good and that you don't have to dress like a gangsta to be successful." Harvey had an ear-to-ear grin on his face.

"So, I guess you don't agree?"

Harvey started, "Nah, man . . . not really. I mean, I get it to a certain extent. There's something to that stuff. In a way, he's right, but my example . . . what I think I have to contribute . . . is my mind and my work habits, not the way I dress. I actually think one of the cool things about being a teacher is that you don't have to wear a tie."

"How about the issue of being a role model for Black students?" I asked.

Harvey paused. Then began, "Again, there's something to it, but the way Doc talks about being Black bothers me. We don't have the same ideas about that."

"About race?"

"Yes, about race." Harvey continued. "Dr. Ferguson actually told me one time that I should stop teaching IB because it's never done anything for Black kids. He told *me* that—*me*. I'm Black! When he said that, I told him that the IB program *in his school* changed my life and that I loved it, but he told me I shouldn't forget about 'my' community. What he meant was that the general education kids were my community because I was Black and I wasn't 'keeping it real' [quotation marks with fingers again] because I was teaching IB. He said that to me one of the first days I was here. Stupid? Insensitive? I don't know but I'm sure he knew I graduated IB."

"Right," I said. "Maybe he wouldn't have said that if he had known."

"Nah . . . " Harvey drawled. "I told him. He just doesn't get it. To Doc, the program is for White kids. That assumption has been around from before he got here and I guess it will be around after. I don't get it, because something like 50% of the teachers and students in the program are actually Black."

"41%," I corrected.

"Whatever," Harvey went on. "The point is that IB made me who I am and it has helped a lot of kids I know, Black, White, and everything else. I resent someone suggesting I'm not connected to my community, because I am. Every Black person in this town is—it's totally Black and White."

"Segregated?" I asked.

"Segregated. Sure," Harvey agreed. "But here's another thing. IB is pretty diverse, but I wouldn't say Doc's argument is totally whack."

"What do you mean?"

Harvey then offered an intriguing insight. "Look at the demographics of the school. IB doesn't mirror the overall population and it doesn't mirror the demographics of the city. So, while IB is diverse . . . *for IB* . . . the kids in the program don't really look like the rest of the school population, so there is something to the idea that it's a program that serves people besides the normal population of the school."

"Hm. That's interesting," I scribbled a note to check this out later. When I was writing that note I noticed another question in the margins of my notepad. "Harvey, another thing I wonder about is this. Anthropologists say that you can essentially talk about race in two ways. The first way is phenotype. That just means the way people look, counting up people by the color of their skin. That's how we know that 41% of the IB program is Black."

"Okay . . . ," Harvey responded, wondering where I was going.

"But the other way is recognizing that race is a sociocultural construct one race invents to oppress another race. Do you think part of Doc's problem with IB is that even though the program is diverse in terms of phenotype, the fact that the program's population isn't like the school or neighborhood's population, he sees it as a tool that advances one race at the expense of another? Could he see the IB program as an instrument of oppression?"

"Whoa, Jeff!" Harvey laughed. "You just went all Ivory Tower on me! What are you talking about?"

Trying to slow down the wheels in my head, I took a deep breath and tried again. "I guess what I mean is similar to what you said. There might be something to Doc's suggestion—and other people's suggestion—that the IB program is a White person's program based on the fact that it doesn't serve the normal population of the school. Even though it's diverse for an IB program, it is much more White than the school."

"And the city," Harvey added.

"Right. I guess what I'm trying to understand is the sociocultural significance of the program. Does it offer possibility and services to Black students that they wouldn't otherwise have or is it something that promotes White people to an inordinate degree?"

Harvey's answer was simple. "It's both, Jeff. There are no simple answers to complicated problems. You can take that from a math teacher."

We spoke about some other things and I thanked Harvey for his time. Late at night and back at home I pored over demographic census data, and some reports from the school's statistical profile. I wrote out a table in my notes (see Table 6.3 on the next page). Starting with the numbers and comparing them made the issues clear but didn't cause any brilliant insights to emerge. Was the IB program "For Whites, By Whites," as Sidney had told me? Yes and no both, seemed to be the answer. Was the program offering opportunities to Black students who otherwise might not have them, as Nat told me and Harvey proved—or full of Black and White students and teachers who were acting White? Again, yes and no, both seemed plausible. Could it be that Doc was onto something in that the program was more White than the school and therefore guilty of some form of institutional racism? I could see it from either side. As I closed my notebook for the evening, I was sure of only one thing. Harvey was right: There are no simple answers to complicated questions.

Table 6.3. Comparative Demographics

	White	Black	Other
City	48	44	8
District	34	55	9
DuBois	12	85	3
IB Program	40	41	19

CHAPTER 7

The Silent Language of Racism

Racism is in our schools—sometimes screaming and sometimes silent. While some are attuned to racism in its covert, obvious forms, few are aware of subtle ways we communicate race and racism to one another. While educational researchers have explored this phenomenon to some extent as part of a hidden curriculum of schooling (Apple, 1990, 1995, 1996; Ladson-Billings, 1998; McLaren, 1993; McLaren & Torres, 1999), few seek to understand the myriad ways race and racism are communicated beyond messages implicit in textbooks (Apple, 1995), through racialized instruction (Delpit, 1995), or racially biased assessment (Darling-Hammond, 1995). Some researchers have documented how avoiding discussions of race is commonplace among educators, and shown that the lack of such conversations severely hampers our ability to challenge a racist status quo of marginalization, discrimination, and exclusion in schools (Tatum, 1999). I certainly saw all of these issues at play in DuBois High School, and as I conducted my research, I filled notebook after notebook with quotes from teachers and administrators explaining various aspects of racism and how they were manifest in the school. However, as in every study of this type, what people actually *did* spoke as loudly as—perhaps even more loudly than—their words. In accordance with the ethnographic approach I took in this study, I was as interested in how people made sense of racism as in how they enacted it. It didn't take long for me to start hearing a silent language of racism that was spoken throughout the school, and I turned to a social theorist outside of education to help make sense of these nonverbal message systems.

THE SILENT LANGUAGE

Anthropologist Edward Hall (1959) identified ten discrete ways cultures express themselves, only one of which is spoken and written language. Collectively considered, these modes of expression constitute a "silent language" by which members and groups in a culture communicate to one another and to others. Hall (1966, 1968, 1977, 1984) identified cultural expression as having these characteristics: interaction, association, subsistence, sexuality, territoriality, temporality, learning, defense, play, and exploitation. What follows is a brief summary of each cultural expression.

- *Interaction* encompasses speech, "which is reinforced by tone of voice and gesture," and writing, "a special form of interaction which uses a particular set of symbols and specially developed forms" (Hall, 1959, p. 38).
- *Association* refers to the way a culture creates and maintains social arrangements, whether these are between two people, a family, or a tribe; association is also manifest through organizational structures, whether these are hierarchical, nonlinear, or dyadic.
- A culture also expresses itself through *subsistence*, "its nutritional requirements" and how it acquires "food in its natural state." Hall (1959) suggested that "not only are people classified and dealt with in terms of their diet, but each society has its own characteristic economy" (p. 40) based on the consumption of foodstuffs.
- The cultural study of *sexuality* examines not only the interactions between men and women, but also the patterns by which gender-specific mores are established and challenged.
- *Territoriality*, which indicates a mode of expression particularly relevant to displaced Native American cultures, is described as "the taking possession, use, and defense of a territory" (Hall, 1959, p. 44).
- *Temporality* deals with the way a culture perceives and relates to time.
- *Learning* entails both formal and informal forms of education and also logics of action and decision making.
- *Play* has to do with the examination of cultural expression via recreation choices, sporting activity, rules of competition, jokes, and the sorts of games children play.
- Cultures express themselves through *defense* when they choose medicinal techniques, conduct warfare, and protect traditions.
- A tenth form, *exploitation*, has to do with the accepted cultural uses of materials and resources, such as land, money, weapons, clothing, housing, transportation, and so on. Due to some overlap in the way I discuss the other forms of cultural communication below, I refrain from discussing exploitation here, and instead will leave that for a future study.

Hall suggested that each of these ten "primary message systems" (PMSs) could be further understood to function in three ways: technically, formally, and informally. Formal aspects of culture are commonly taught by guided instruction and admonition. These are the commonly accepted norms and behaviors of a culture reinforced by most cultural members. Informal cultural aspects are those unspoken mores in a culture of which members may not even be aware, but to which they adhere nonetheless. Technical aspects of a culture are essentially expressions of skill, practiced over generations or developed to meet a novel challenge. In a break with the way narratives drive the organization of most chapters in this book, here I will present evidence related to each primary message system to explore the ways the silent language worked at DuBois.

INTERACTION

In discussing the first, and perhaps most obvious, form of cultural communication, Hall (1959) wrote:

> One of the most highly elaborated forms of interaction is speech, which is reinforced by tone of voice and gesture. Writing is a special form of interaction which uses a particular set of symbols and specially developed forms. In addition to the well-known linguistic interaction there are specialized versions for each PMS . . . teaching, learning, play, and defense also represent specialized forms of interaction. (p 38)

So, when we consider interaction as a way of communicating culture, we include writing, reading, speech, tone of voice, and gesture. I won't focus on this here, as nearly every chapter in this book focuses on these various forms of interaction, but one aspect of this in particular bears some attention here: gesture and body language.

At DuBois it was common for teachers, administrators, and students to be critical of one another's gestures and body language. Importantly, these critiques were different when leveled at members of one's own race rather than another. Examples of such interactions included:

- A White assistant principal routinely criticized Black students for "not standing up straight," "walking like a gangsta," or "walking like a pimp" as he stood in the hallways between classes. He made no such comments to White students, although they often assumed similar postures.

- Certain White teachers repeatedly told students to sit up rather than slouch in their seats during instruction. Often, White teachers would walk past several White students sitting in a reclined position to correct Black students who were not sitting fully erect.
- White teachers often derided Black students when they presented in front of the class for not making eye contact with the audience. Although observation data suggested that just as many White students presented this way, it was rare to see a White student admonished for this behavior.
- In an effort to connect to Black students culturally, younger White teachers and administrators often crossed their arms, made "gang signs," and said things like, "yo, yo, yo." They routinely followed this behavior by laughing and smiling, which Black students rarely did after such interactions. There was a pronounced difference of perspective on this among White teachers, some of whom explained that they needed to do this to reach out to students in this way to show their cultural relevance, and others who explained that they would not (in the words of three experienced White teachers) "act Black because we work in a Black school."

Interestingly, Black teachers and administrators also singled out Black students to "correct" them more than White students.

- It was common to see Black teachers urge Black students to alter their body language. One teacher in particular routinely admonished his students for "walking like a thug," while another Black teacher told her students nearly every day that they wouldn't get a job unless they "acted more professionally," which meant "standing up straight, wearing your pants in the right place on your waist, and carrying yourself like a CEO, not like a hustler."
- Black administrators in the school routinely encouraged Black teachers and students to carry themselves in a professional manner, meaning stand up straight, dress appropriately, and speak in a subdued voice, in case the (primarily White) administrators from the district were to come by.

White and Black educators and students communicated with one another through gesture and body language. The nature of this communication and the message varied depending on whether the interaction was within or across racial groups, but it was clear that this form of interaction was used to keep people within certain cultural expectations and to manage the group image projected to other subcultures.

ASSOCIATION

Schools are places where hierarchical and bureaucratic organizational structures define professional relationships and establish "chains of command" that dictate that certain people in schools communicate frequently and others seldom associate with one another. Moreover, the nature of people's associations in the school is clearly defined to the extent that there are certain expectations for teachers when associating with other teachers. This was distinct, however, from the ways in which teachers associated with administrators, students, parents, or support staff.

Additionally, race helped to shape associations between people throughout the school community, primarily through informal associations. White administrators and Black administrators each engaged in a form of code-shifting when associating with members of their own race and members of another race. This dynamic also shifted depending on (a) who was in the room at the time, and (b) what position they occupied in the hierarchy of the district. In large groups of mixed race, it was common for people throughout the organization to associate in a manner commensurate with their position in the formal hierarchy of the school system. That is, students would be proper, respectful, and deferential to teachers, who in turn would associate in a like manner with administrators. It was common, for example, for students to call teachers "Mr. Jones" or "Ms. Johnson" when an administrator was present, even if they addressed that teacher by first name in the classroom. This dynamic held when the size of the group decreased, but changed when the racial composition of the group became more homogeneous, regardless of hierarchical position. That is, the Blacker or Whiter a group became, regardless of size, the less formal it became in the way that members interacted. In many instances, racially homogeneous groups exhibited a kind of racial solidarity, which came with both a loosening of formality and a willingness to engage more difficult-to-discuss issues related to education, including not only race but also gender, sexuality, spirituality, poverty, and many other sociocultural dynamics related to education. In a sense, large, mixed-race groups of educators had norms of silence, where smaller, racially homogeneous groups of educators had norms of open communication. Given themes and incidents discussed elsewhere in this book, it seems reasonable to infer that this dynamic can be attributed to several reasons but is due at least partially to the real or perceived threat of racism.

SUBSISTENCE

A culture is defined in part by what its people eat and how they obtain what they eat. Likewise, various subcultures are "classified and dealt with in terms of their diet" (Hall, 1959, p. 40) and sorted into social classes. During one of my first interviews with a White administrator, he told me something I found quite incredible: "The cafeteria at DuBois High School serves fried chicken every day." When I asked why that was, he replied:

> They have other stuff too, of course, hamburgers and fries and such, but there's always fried chicken. It's been like that for years. And, it's not only the cafeteria—we have it at every school function where we serve food. When we have a parents' day, there's fried chicken. When we do an awards dinner, there's fried chicken. When we do an open house, there's fried chicken. For fundraisers, most of the clubs sell fried chicken coupons. In fact, at those school functions it's always fried chicken and red Kool-Aid. Years ago, before I was here, we tried to do a spaghetti dinner just for something different and no one came. We switched back to fried chicken and the entire school and everyone's cousins were there.

I responded by asking, "Okay, but do you realize the racist stereotypes associated with that?"

"Of course I do," he responded. "There's a lot of truth in most of those stereotypes. You may not like it—hell, I like it less than you, because I've got to eat it all the time—but I got to get parents' butts in those seats. They expect it now, and I'll be damned if I'm going to be the one to let them down just because someone might think it's racist."

Black administrators and teachers had different perspectives. The following quotes illustrate some of these views:

- "I mean, how much more racist can you get—they serve chicken and watermelon at every school-sanctioned event."
- "I don't go near the cafeteria—that chicken smells like racism."
- "I like chicken, but come on—given the racial problems in this school, how can they keep serving it at faculty retreats?"

- ". . . seriously, how can they serve what they serve in the cafeteria? The kids see that, and they're not stupid—they know what it means—they know what it says about the White people who run this school!"
- "I've requested something different to eat at school events, but they keep serving chicken. It's like they want to keep slapping us in the face in every possible way."

Another interesting form of social stratification was evident in relation to subsistence. Although students and faculty were prohibited from leaving school grounds during lunch, administrators left the campus nearly every day. It was common for administrators to walk the halls of DuBois with 32-ounce soda cups emblazoned with the bright colors of local fast food chains. These cups were a visible reminder of the school's power dynamics and hierarchical governance structures, and even if it wasn't intended that way, those soda cups were a tangible reminder of who was in charge—a badge of privilege to those who worked and studied at the school.

SEXUALITY

Hall (1959) noted that "all cultures differentiate between men and women, and usually when a given behavior pattern becomes associated with one sex it will then be dropped by the other" (p. 41), and so it was at DuBois High School. Interestingly, there were significant differences between the ways that gender played out within the Black and White leadership subcultures. In an earlier article published using these data, my colleague Gaetane Jean-Marie and I explored some of these gender differences (Brooks & Jean-Marie, 2007) in greater depth. In short, we found that within the White leadership culture of the school, women tended to defer to men, even when the men occupied positions below women in the organization. Alternatively, in the Black leadership culture, women operated as men's moral compass, guiding them on key decisions and keeping them in line when needed.

TERRITORIALITY

Territoriality is the technical term used by ethologists to describe the taking possession, use, and defense of a territory. To have a territory is to have one of the essential components of life; to lack one is one of the most precarious of all conditions. Status, for example, is indicated by the distance one sits from the head of the table on formal occasions (Hall, 1959, p. 45).

The physical layout of DuBois High School, and where teachers were placed, reinforced the hierarchical social and professional structure of the school. Moreover, these distributions of space reflected the divided nature of the school along racial lines. As in many other high schools, administrators at DuBois assigned teachers to particular rooms based on a constellation of factors that included seniority, the subject they taught, and proximity to other resources germane to educational programming (i.e., the classrooms of language arts and social studies teachers who shared instructional resources might be located near one another). However, mapping race onto the DuBois room assignments revealed that teachers were largely clustered together by race: Black teachers with Black teachers and White teachers with White teachers. Moreover, these racial blocks of classrooms had differential resources as well. For example, one block included several Black teachers, one of whom in particular who was very close to Principal Ferguson. This teacher, and indeed all teachers whose rooms were located immediately adjacent to hers, had relatively new furniture, computers, and instructional materials. Other blocks of teachers, particularly White teachers, were not so well supported but in many instances had created their own stashes of materials funded by alternative means. In a sense, an underground economy of instructional resources grew of necessity. Reviewing the classroom assignments for the 4 years prior to the study suggested that Black teachers also stayed in their classrooms longer and had larger and more desirable spaces, regardless of seniority, than White teachers.

TEMPORALITY

There were striking differences between the ways that Black and White educators in DuBois viewed time. White educators in particular often expressed an impatience that drove them to great frustration with regard to many educational processes and outcomes. The following quotes illustrate this value:

- "I can't wait for the implementation to run its course. Even though I know it takes a while for change to take hold and work, we don't have time. I need results now."
- "I feel a sense of urgency that many of my colleagues don't feel."
- "The scores in math and reading are showing progress, but we need huge gains and we need them yesterday."

- "I'm a change agent. I'm here to shake things up and make things happen ASAP. I don't have time and I don't have patience for people who just make excuses."

Black educators, on the other hand, showed a great deal more patience and an understanding that for educational change to take hold, it would take, among other things, a great deal of time, sustained progress, and steady change.

- "The system's been screwed up for a long time, so it will take a long time to fix."
- "There are no silver bullets, no quick-fix solutions to all of this."
- "We need to stop focusing on year-to-year gains and benchmarks; that is distracting us from the fact that real change takes years, even decades, to take hold."
- "If you try to reform a school at 100 miles an hour, you can't focus on what's right in front of you. We need that focus."
- "No matter how fast or furious we try to change what's happening in the school, if we're out of sync with what's happening in the community, it won't work. The school needs to move at the same speed as the community."

To be sure, there were variations within each race, but these quotes are illustrative of strong subcultural norms. When races interacted, the plenum largely espoused the White approach to time. For example, when time was discussed at faculty meetings or as part of the revision of the School Improvement Plan, the group consensus viewed time as running out and took the approach that everything must be treated with the utmost urgency.

LEARNING

In *The Silent Language* (1959) Hall observed:

> People reared in different cultures *learn to learn* differently and go about the process of acquiring culture in their own way. Some do so by memory and rote without reference to "logic" as we think of it, while some learn by demonstration. . . . The fact is, however, that once people have learned to learn in a given way it is extremely hard for them to learn in any other way. This is because, in the process of learning they have acquired a long set of tacit conditions and assumptions in which learning is imbedded. (p. 48)

These observations were very much in line with the notion that there were two distinct racial subcultures at DuBois High School, and that members of each learned differently. It became clear early in the study that Black educators and White educators learned in different ways, both formally and informally.

Among White educators, there was an emphasis on learning information, and on being able to recite key names and facts from memory. There was a sense among these educators, even those few who professed a postmodern perspective on their work, that there was one perfect way of educating that hadn't yet been discovered. There was a tacit belief that "good teaching" as a monolithic and immutable endeavor actually existed and lay somewhere ahead, just out of their reach. By and large, White educators seemed happier with professional development when they walked out of the session with a concrete product or strategy they could use in their classrooms the next day. Black educators, on the other hand, placed a much greater emphasis on informal learning and on forming praxis from what one teacher called "book learning" and "real-world learning." For this teacher, real-world learning meant "that knowledge has to work in multiple contexts. It has to work in the classroom, it has to work in the lunchroom, it has to work at home and it has to have relevance in the community." In opposition, book learning had not as much bearing.

PLAY

The study of school culture generally has ignored the concept of play. However, looking at the way educators played provided interesting insights into how Black and White leadership cultures at the school were different. One obvious form of playfulness occurred between races. Nearly all of the Black educators at the school had earned their teaching degrees at a nearby large historically Black university, while most of the White faculty members had attended the much larger state university. They engaged in ongoing banter and lighthearted rivalry about which school's sports teams were better, which school's academic programs were better, and even which school had the best traditions and parties.

Beyond these shared experiences, there was evidence within the school that Black educators and White educators joked and played differently, and did so in different spaces. As Hall (1959) pointed out, "there are places and times for play" (p. 51), and these were different for each racial subculture at the school. White educators tended to joke at the beginning of faculty meetings and then work quickly toward a sustained, serious tone. Likewise, conversations before school and at the end of the day were often full of levity, but throughout the course of the day there was a general business-only tone to interactions. Black educators tended to be more serious and guarded in faculty meetings, laughing if a joke was initiated but not offering one themselves. Black educators tended to be more guarded in this respect and, as one Black teacher explained, "I don't want people here to accuse me of being lazy. If I tell a joke, rumors will start that I'm screwing around and not doing my job. White folks can tell jokes—it's more dangerous for Black people." Play, therefore, was yet another marker of differentiation between Black and White teachers both in and out of school.

DEFENSE

The idea of being guarded carried over to the concept of defense, which Hall (1959) defined as behavior driven by the need to protect "not only against potentially hostile forces in nature but against those within human society" (p. 53). Hall's understanding of defense moved beyond this need for self-protection and looked inward to include "the destructive forces within their own persons" (p. 53) and the unique place of religion in "warding off both the dangers in nature and within the individual" (p. 53). Defense in schools, then, takes many forms. It can be manifest as guarding one's career; one's personal space; and one's mental, spiritual, and physical well-being.

When considered in relation to race, educators at DuBois exhibited many forms of defense. The most obvious was a form of racialized closed-door autonomy (Lortie, 1975). It was common around the school to pass by rooms of teachers conferring, all of whom were either all-White or all-Black. These meetings were nearly always with educational pretense: discussing curriculum, personnel, discipline, the needs of certain students, and so on. However, it was impossible to ignore that these informal meetings occurred largely behind closed doors and almost always in groups with racial homogeneity.

CONCLUSION

While the interviews I conducted with these teachers were insightful and revealing, there were many other modes of communicating race and racism that went unspoken. Looking at issues of race in the school through the silent language framework illuminated many subtle dynamics that contribute to the racial dynamics in the school. This area of race studies demands more attention, but this initial exploration of the approach was extremely helpful in understanding the pervasive nature of race and racism in the school's culture. It seems clear that there are many nonverbal languages used in the practice of leadership and in the communication of racism in schools. Future studies that explore how these messages are communicated and how they are received may suggest important insights about the way we prepare and practice leadership and undo racism in schools.

CHAPTER 8

Educational Misleadership

Over the course of the 2 years I studied DuBois High School, it was clear that educators at the school engaged in as much misleadership as leadership, and that this behavior was shaped at least partially by racial dynamics. One of the most accepted definitions of leadership is to think of it as the art and science of influencing a group of people toward a common goal (Northouse, 2010). Misleadership, then, is behaviors that prevent the attainment of goals, or that prioritize individual goals over group goals. As I amassed data on behavior, they loosely fell into four themes: (1) incompetence, (2) indifference and apathy, (3) avoidance, and (4) unethical behavior. To be sure, there were other forms of leadership behavior, but they either were less developed or are explored in other chapters of this book. Further, it is important to point out that I focused primarily on aspects of these themes where race, race relations, and/or racism were evident, implicitly or explicitly. Sadly, I have seen plenty of this behavior over the past decade during my studies of school leadership. I feel the themes discussed in this chapter are among the most common reasons leadership does not have the influence it might in the education of children and the work of adults in schools. Educational leadership, conceived as I describe it here, could fill a book by itself. However, as it is not the central focus of this study, I will leave an in-depth exploration of these concepts for another time.

INCOMPETENCE

There were many instances of professional incompetence among leaders at DuBois High School. I witnessed basic incompetence related to not knowing school and district procedures, as well as to content knowledge and pedagogical acumen, on a weekly basis. This was due partially to the high turnover of teachers at the school, frequent changes in these policies, and the fact that there was a generally low level of accountability at the school, for either educational processes or outcomes. Put differently, educators seldom were held responsible for incompetence. This lack of accountability extended so far that basic credentials required to assume teaching and administrative positions at the school frequently were waived or ignored so that favored people could be put in specific positions. Interestingly, in every instance, these arranged appointments were created by someone for a member of the person's own race. One teacher, Tabitha, described a situation where the Black principal had created quasi-administrative positions for three Black teachers in the school:

"Did you know [Dean] Ken Johnson is on a half-day appointment?"

"No. What is that? I've never heard of a half-day appointment."

"It's when someone has a partial instructional assignment and a partial administrative assignment. So it's sort of split appointment."

"Okay. That's common, right?"

"Well, it would be if that's what he was really doing, but have you ever seen him teach a class? He's not doing the other half of his job. Other teachers are covering his classes so he doesn't have to teach. There are four other people with that kind of assignment in this school. Three are Black and one is White."

"What does race have to do with it?"

"The three Black teachers don't teach any classes. They have cushy half-time administrative responsibilities with essentially no responsibility. The White guy on a half-day teaches a full load, *and* he has administrative responsibilities."

"Okay, but is that a coincidence? Do you think it really has anything to do with race?"

Tabitha leaned back in her chair, sized me up with her eyes, and then leaned forward and said, "Look—it's about race. I was in a meeting a few months ago and the principal pointed to those three as examples of the kinds of leaders we need in our schools. They are three of the least accomplished educators in the school and he's hand-picked them for these quasi-administrative positions. They all got raises and they're all taking their administrative certification courses right now, except for Ken. Do you know why he doesn't have his certification?"

"No, why?" asked.

"He finished his coursework. He doesn't have it because he's failed the certification examination nine times."

I taught in an administrator certification program, and I knew our students passed over 95% of the time. By all accounts the examination was terribly easy. "Nine times? Are you sure?"

"Absolutely. I have a friend at the state department of education—it's true. On top of that, the superintendent has told everyone who will listen that as soon as he passes the exam he will be a principal in the district. It's completely insane. The guy is totally incompetent."

Something wasn't sitting well with me. "But, Tabitha, why are you saying it's about race? Couldn't this just be him protecting his friends, or maybe he really does think Ken has a lot of potential."

Tabitha frowned at me. "Come on, Jeff, you've seen him in action. Have you ever seen him actually do work? He's supposed to be a dean, but the assistant principal in charge of curriculum does the schedule and handles all academic matters. The department chairs do the School Improvement Plan. He even has other people stand in for him at district-level meetings. I mean, seriously, I've never seen him working."

While Tabitha, a White teacher, surely offered her insights based on a limited understanding of the situation of three Black teachers, there were multiple examples of such arranged appointments. There were also numerous instances of White teachers and administrators being placed at DuBois by White central office personnel before their qualifications were entirely in order.

Another clear case of incompetence relates to the school's budget. It was clear that many administrators and teachers did not know basic regulations, principles, and procedures of budgeting. While it is possible that some of this was due to genuine confusion, ignorance, or intentional deceit, it was obvious in many cases that people throughout the school—people who had access to the school's funds—did not understand how the budget worked. As one administrator explained:

> At first I thought everyone was trying to embezzle or misappropriate funds intentionally. The more I worked with people around issues related to the budget I realized that most of them honestly don't have a clue how to balance funds or coordinate the various lines of a budget. They aren't trying to do anything illegal, they are just clueless, and that's scary!

That said, there was consensus among teachers at the school that if you wanted something that required funds, you needed to speak to someone with budget authority who shared your race. Whether or not it was acted upon, there was consensus that leaders looked out for members of their race and prioritized distribution of funds based in large part on racial affinity.

Another pronounced form of incompetence related to a general lack of knowledge regarding instructional methods and content. The first school-wide event I attended was a faculty work meeting dedicated to revising and updating the School Improvement Plan. At this meeting it was clear that several administrators and teachers had developed the skill of using buzzwords without understanding what they meant. After an address to the entire faculty, they split up into working teams to focus on different parts of the report. I first sat with a curriculum group, who used basic terms like *scope, sequence, horizontal alignment, vertical alignment,* and *reading across content areas.* The principal, who at the time was sitting next to me, got up to walk away from the group and was asked why. Laughing, he exclaimed, "I don't understand any of this newfangled stuff! I'll leave this work to the experts."

A few minutes later, I joined the instructional methods group, where the principal was then sitting. They were engaged in an interesting and lively conversation about the challenges of different instructional approaches, such as direct instruction, differentiated instruction, ability grouping, and inclusion of special-needs students. As often happens in high schools, the conversation centered on how various content areas approached these differently. As I sat down with the group, the principal leaned over and touched the elbow of a teacher next to him and whispered, "I have no idea what you all are talking about, but it's great stuff!" At the time I wasn't sure if he was serious or just deferring to the content experts in the group. However, teachers repeatedly explained that the principal, whose teaching experience had been 2 years of physical education instruction in a middle school, had little knowledge of content or pedagogy, and actually showed little interest in the subject. One teacher spoke for many when she explained, "I have no respect for the guy as an instructional leader. He has no knowledge of, or interest in, what I'm doing." It was unclear exactly how race played a role in this, but it was striking to me that White teachers more often criticized the principal for his lack of instructional leadership, while Black teachers seldom critiqued him in this manner.

INDIFFERENCE AND APATHY

Apathy and indifference were evident among many educators at Du-Bois High School. These were manifest with regard to various aspects of school, specifically on individual and interpersonal levels. Four distinct forms of indifference and apathy recurred throughout the 2 years of the study: (1) educators not learning students', teachers', and parents' names; (2) administrators moving teachers around the building and changing their teaching assignments arbitrarily; (3) the principal falling asleep during teacher observations; and (4) educators not attending extracurricular events.

At DuBois High School there were several instances where educators did not take the time to get to know one another, the students, or parents.

One particularly embarrassing incident occurred when two students won National Merit Awards. In the past, an administrator had presented these in front of the student body at the year-end awards ceremony. However, the first year of this study the awards were not given because no administrator could pronounce the students' names, one of whom was Kenyan and the other Japanese. That this was due to indifference or apathy was highlighted when a new assistant principal arrived at the school the second year into the study and learned every student's and teacher's name by the end of October. Likewise, it was common for teachers to not know one another's names, their students' names, and the names of their students' parents. To be sure, some teachers knew all of their students early in the year, but even in March it was commonplace that classroom teachers would ask students what their names were. While the examples above are somewhat exceptional illustrations of a pervasive issue, it was clear that, generally speaking, Black educators were much more likely to know the names of Black students, teachers, and parents, and White teachers were more likely to know the names of White students, teachers, and parents.

Another form of indifference involved administrators moving teachers around the building and changing their teaching assignments arbitrarily. One teacher explained to me a situation that occurred with the school's Latin teacher, who left the summer in the middle of my study:

"The [assistant principal for curriculum] was going to move him and . . . they don't understand how much that upset him. And the irony of it is that the AP who did it is now gone himself! That's just so crazy to me that you have these people that want to come in and, just without asking a teacher if they want to, implement all these changes based on nothing, except maybe race, since teachers seem to be clustered that way throughout the school. Really, though, it is based on probably a misunderstanding of what these teachers actually do. It's an attitude about teachers, like we're chess pieces. One size fits all. We're not even chess pieces—they are specialized—more like we're checkers. Where every piece does the same thing.

"And they have no understanding of what that did. I remember the day that teacher came down and he said that they essentially had taken his room. And their explanation to me later was that it's a big old room, nobody really likes it, he'll be happy to be somewhere else. They never asked him. He loved the room. It was huge. He could do all sorts of things. He had closets with all his lessons organized and ready to go. Not only were they going to move him, but because he's certified to teach reading in addition to Latin, they were going to make him teach remedial reading to sophomores. Now this is a guy who is our only Latin teacher and teaches five preps. He's on a high level, a different level. He's one of the few Latin teachers in the district."

"So, how did they plan to cover those classes?" I asked.

They were going to move the philosophy teacher and just assign Latin to Maggie Reynolds, who's a psychology teacher, because she took a Latin class in college. So, for no apparent reason you had two miserable teachers. And all for what? Nobody said to them, here's an idea. What do you think of it?"

"Right," I agreed.

"It's as though we have no feelings, no expertise. So instead of having an outstanding Latin teacher, now we have no Latin teacher. What's more, Maggie is in over her head, and I think she's going to leave at the end of the year."

Which, I note, she did.

Indifference and apathy also took place in the form of an instance of the principal falling asleep during a teaching observation. This seemed to me a one-time incident when a teacher mentioned it for the first time. However, it assumed much greater importance in that more than 75% of the interviewees mentioned this event to illustrate how little the principal was concerned with teachers in general, and with instruction in particular. There was little to suggest that the incident itself had anything to do with race, since the principal and observed teacher were both Black. However, what was interesting about the incident was the way that Black and White teachers interpreted the event. White teachers overwhelmingly suggested that falling asleep during the observation was the ultimate slap in the face to the school's teachers. As one White teacher put it, while pounding his fist on the desk, "That shows me he has no respect for us, for kids, and for education! It's SO UNPROFESSIONAL!" Black teachers, on the other hand, were by and large more forgiving, noting that there had been a basketball game the night before and that he was under quite a lot of stress at the time. A Black teacher explained it by shrugging and saying, "You know what, we've all wanted to put our head down on the desk out of exhaustion at times. The lesson was probably boring anyway."

AVOIDANCE

Avoidance, simply not engaging in leadership by removing oneself, was a consistent tactic of DuBois High School leaders. The most common forms of avoidance were: (1) leaving the building for long periods of time/ leaving early; (2) delegating substantive responsibilities; (3) not looking at data that contradict assumptions; and (4) not doing end-of-year evaluations. It appeared that avoidance was indiscriminate with regard to race, race relations, or racism, yet it is worth noting that avoidance was very prevalent at the school. Educational administrators routinely left for long periods of the day without anyone knowing where they were. This may have gone largely unnoticed in a school with a principal and three assistant principals, but given that teachers and students were prohibited from leaving during the school day, the fact that administrators were not accountable in this regard was a source of annoyance for students and teachers. This led in turn to a great many rumors circulating that administrators were cheating on their spouses, taking leisurely lunches, or just going home early. Even though it was fairly common that administrators were either at district administrative meetings, in professional development sessions, or meeting with other educational stakeholders about school concerns, there was generally one administrator off-site at all times. Administrators also delegated quite a lot of duties, which exacerbated the tensions that developed between administrators and teachers.

In addition, teachers commonly complained that administrators would not look at data they had either generated or analyzed that suggested certain dynamics in the school regarding instruction, curriculum, or efficiency. They also complained that there was no formal end-of-year evaluation. Instead of the summative performance evaluation teachers were promised as part of their contract, they simply had to sign a form indicating that they had had such a meeting before they could pick up their final paycheck.

UNETHICAL BEHAVIOR

Other chapters of this book detail forms of unethical behavior, but three forms not described elsewhere are worth noting, as they allow for a more holistic perspective on the context. Sexual harassment and cronyism did appear to be influenced by racial dynamics. Lying, the third form of unethical behavior discussed here, was blatant and obvious.

Women at DuBois High School often mentioned that they either had been victims of sexual harassment or had heard of other teachers experiencing sexual harassment. White women were more forthcoming discussing this with me, although several Black women also indicated after several interviews that they had experienced sexual harassment. One White teacher, Tabitha Sorensen, explained her experience:

"You know Dean Johnson, right?"

"Sure," I responded. I had interviewed Ken twice, and mentioned that he seemed like a nice enough man.

"Seriously?" she asked sarcastically. "That guy is a sexist pig and he constantly harasses women on this campus."

"Sexual harassment?" I thought back on some of my experiences with Ken. In fact, I had heard him make several entirely inappropriate comments during the study. There were two Black teaching interns working at the school the first year I was there, and whenever they passed in the hallway he made awful comments about what he would do to, and with, them if he weren't married. He even said once that it didn't matter that he was married. He just wanted to get them alone. He made these comments only in the presence of other male administrators, who generally laughed and rolled their eyes. I interviewed Ken as part of this study, and during the interview he inquired as to whether I had interviewed those two women. When I told him I couldn't tell him that due to confidentiality concerns, he told me he just wanted to know if they liked him. He then said that if I was still going to interview either of them, he would like for me to find out if they liked him. I'll never forget the look on his face when he leaned in close to me, winked, and said, "You know, I want to know if they *like* me." It was terribly uncomfortable and it put me at a crossroads. In studies like this, you try to build rapport with people at the school, but Ken's repeated sexist remarks offended me and I felt that this request crossed the line. I ended the interview then and there and told him I thought what he asked was totally out of order. He looked disappointed and told me that he "thought I was one of his boys." He asked me to delete the interview, told me he was joking, and asked me not to tell anyone. I didn't answer, but he stood there and watched me delete the file before he left the room.

Tabitha continued, "So, Ken is in line to get promoted. All he does is stare at women's asses, and nobody on this faculty that I know of has any respect for him as a human being. He is gross. He says really sexist things. Have you ever heard him? He drools at the interns. They'll come and talk to the administrators about something or walk by them in the hall, and the second they're out of earshot, you have to listen to all this totally sexist, unbearably degrading stuff. They do it when I'm standing right there— not just Ken, there are a whole lot of them. They have no clue that it's degrading to the interns, to me, and to all women. They don't care—I think they know they're untouchable. Haven't you seen them do that?"

"I have."

"And what did you do about it?"

"I listened to it a few times and then I asked him to stop."

"And did he?"

"Yes, he hasn't said anything around me since."

She thought about that.

"Well, you should put that in your study. Sexual harassment is a constant issue in high schools, though you rarely see anything out there about it. The most we get is an annual sexual harassment training video that everyone laughs at and makes sexist remarks about when we're watching."

"Okay," I answered meekly, not sure exactly how to respond and questioning whether I had responded properly to the men I heard speak that way around the school.

"I've put up with so much of it over the years. I've been a victim and I've watched women who were victims throw away their careers or give in to these men's advances. It's an awful unspoken part of working in a school like this. And, though I'm sure you're not convinced, it is totally about race."

"How do you mean?" I asked.

"There are different norms in the Black and White communities about what is acceptable and what isn't in terms of how men treat women. These guys are vipers and they get excited when there's a young Black woman in the room. We had a young Black woman intern here this year, Pauline Kameni, who was gorgeous. Did you meet her?"

"I did."

"Well, she was working in guidance last fall. The principal hit on her twice and the dean hit on her another time. She came to the department chair, the lead guidance counselor, and complained. He's a Black man, and Pauline hadn't been around long enough to know that they are all friends from way back. Anyway, she didn't know what to do because here she is, an intern. She wants to keep the job, right? That has happened again and again and again at this school. I mean it's been happening for years—decades.

"So, Pauline told her cooperating teacher Nicole, and Nicole wasn't supposed to tell anybody but she told me because she didn't know what to say. I gave Pauline some basic advice, but I rarely saw her after that. She made herself very scarce. At the time I didn't even know if she finished her internship. Later I found out she quit, and left teaching altogether. I don't know where she ran. I don't know what ever happened to her, but that is wrong. It's horrible. And don't you think she'll tell other people who might be coming here? The sad thing about it isn't PR, though; it's that many of us—especially when we are younger—get harassed by administrators, other teachers, and students constantly. It isn't all about race, but there's a racial tension there. I'm White and don't know everything about it, but there's a different meaning to gender relationships in the Black community."

I noted that after the interview described above, I asked participants about sexual harassment in several follow-up interviews. It was among the most taboo topics and one they were most uncomfortable trying to address. I eventually refrained from asking participants about this, instead noting that sexual harassment is both an underdeveloped theme in this study and a huge but important gap in educational research. I also noted that during this study, two DuBois teachers were sentenced to time in jail for sexual-harassment-related charges. There were also a great number of sexual-harassment-related student issues, almost none of which were formally documented.

Lying was common, although I found it not overtly influenced by racial dynamics. Teachers often mentioned that they had been lied to and that a culture of lying was evident throughout the school. Many teachers felt that administrators in particular lied to them constantly and that it undermined trust in the school community. Some typical comments included:

- "The administration doesn't follow through when they say they will do something. It's been like that for years."
- "I can't count the number of times the administrators have lied to my face. There's more solidarity among teachers . . . and maybe greater trust among administrators, but I don't count on the administration. I'm on my own here."
- "I've been promised so many things! More resources, more time, specialized professional development. None of it happens. The amazing thing is that it's so common that no one bothers to hold them accountable anymore. It's just accepted that they will lie to us."
- "You can't trust the administrators to tell you the truth. They have their motives and agendas and they have nothing to do with supporting teachers. I can't tell you how many times I've been told one thing, then I go down the hall and my colleagues have been told something else. It's frustrating, but they don't seem to have much of a conscience about it. It doesn't bother the administrators around here."

Again, participants were hesitant to suggest that race played a role in lying in the school. However, given the fact that many correlated lying highly with trust, and nearly all participants suggested they trusted members of their own race more than those of another, it seems this may be another area of educational misleadership that bears further investigation.

*   *   *

There are many forms of misleadership, but those documented in this chapter are specifically related to racism. It is clear that many decisions in the school that should have been made based on educational data were made instead based on discrimination, stereotype, misinformation, and assumption.

Part III

LESSONS LEARNED AND POSSIBILITIES FOR THE FUTURE

CHAPTER 9

Moving Toward a New Educational Leadership

The twofold purpose of this chapter is to reflect on key findings from Du-Bois High School and to stimulate reflection, discourse, and changes in practice around issues of race and racism in educational leadership among researchers, graduate students, teachers, and administrators. Throughout this book I have drawn from research on social foundations of education, educational leadership, sociology, and anthropology to understand the relationship between racism and educational leadership, particularly in schools of mixed cultures like DuBois. To this end, this chapter selectively explores particular points grounded in this research, and that have prompted me to rethink and change the way I engage and ignore these issues in my own teaching, service, and research.

As I have mentioned elsewhere, these topics are changing constantly and to some extent are context-specific. However, the succinct nature of a book chapter has advantages; it is an excellent vehicle for starting conversations with colleagues, students, and leaders, who then can begin a more substantive and sustained dialogue through their own work. I offer this chapter as a tool to help you reflect on your own attitudes, assumptions, and behaviors, and also as a tool to initiate conversations with your colleagues that eventually might lead to action.

RACISM INFLUENCES LEADERSHIP PRACTICE

This research suggested that racism occurred in many forms in the school and that it influenced the practice of leadership activity. This is in line with previous research that also suggests that racism influences educational leadership (e.g., Brooks & Jean-Marie, 2007; Brown, 2005; Capper, 1993; Gooden, 2005; Horsford, 2010; Jackson, 1988; Scheurich & Skrla, 2003; Tillman, 2002; Young & Laible, 2000). Throughout the book there are numerous examples of White privilege influencing instruction, administrative decisions, and curricula. There are examples of decisions that should be guided by data being made instead based on racial prejudice and discrimination. There are instances where teachers and administrators showed favor based on race, denied services to students and to one another because of race, and where race was a factor in educational outcomes like discipline referrals, special education referrals, and expulsions. This basic finding demands that educators working in schools reconsider the way they engage—and ignore—issues of race in their schools. This research underscores that this school did not operate in a post-racial society. Rather, educational processes and outcomes were highly racialized and inequitable. Students and educators lose when issues of race are ignored, swept under the rug, or avoided.

The Definition of Race Is Contested, and Is by Nature Constantly Under Revision

On May 17, 1998, the American Anthropological Association (AAA) adopted its Statement on "Race" (http://www.aaanet.org/stmts/racepp. htm). While I urge you to explore the AAA position in depth, and think about what it says about race, I also urge you to reflect on what it embodies —a strong and research-based political statement formulated by one of the most highly respected social science organizations in the world. Should educational leadership scholars representing organizations such as universities, preparation programs, and international organizations like the University Council for Educational Administration (UCEA) and Division A of the American Educational Research Association (AERA) likewise seek to develop such statements? I'm suggesting we go beyond platitudes about educating the whole child to more explicitly focus on oppressive social forces such as racism, ageism, sexism, ableism, poverty, classism, and so on. Interestingly, the most widely adopted set of state standards, the Interstate School Leaders Licensure Consortium Standards for School Leaders, does not contain the word *race*. The Educational Leadership Constituent Council Standards for Advanced Programs in Educational Leadership, endorsed by the National Policy Board for Educational Administration, include race under the "culture" standard, but "race" does not appear in any other standard. Of course, one can take a position only when one is able to articulate that position.

The AAA statement essentially asserts that there are two fundamental concepts that should frame our understanding of race. The first of these fundamental concepts is that *race can be studied in terms of phenotypic difference.* Phenotype is the way a demographer might study race; that is, counting the number of people who are identified, or self-identify, as a particular racial affiliation. In terms of educational leadership, it is important to note a basic inequity in the phenotypic distribution of school leaders in relation to students in the United States. I presented data on this topic in Chapter 1, but it is worth revisiting here. The 2003–2004 School and Staffing Survey estimated the total distribution of "minority" principals in public schools at 17.6%, although the country's minority student population was estimated at 39.7% (Strizek, Pittsonberger, Riordan, Lyter, & Orlofsky, 2006). Moreover, research suggests that instead of increasing, the number of school administrators of color actually may have declined over the past several decades (Gay, 1997). Why might this be? And what are the intended and unintended consequences of such trends and distributions for schools and children? What is the phenotypic distribution of students, teachers, and leaders in your educational organizations, both now and over time? Do you know what it looks like now? Do you know the history of these trends at your institution? Why, or why not?

The second fundamental concept in the AAA Statement on "Race" is that *race is a culturally constructed phenomenon used for the purpose of oppression.* Suggesting that race is a culturally constructed instrument of oppression is to acknowledge that people have a long and terrible tradition of using the concept of racial inequality to create dominant and subordinate groups. Given an enormous corpus of multidisciplinary research on organizational culture that documents the influence of culture on leadership practice in all manner of institutions, it is incumbent on educational leadership scholars and practitioners to understand the ways leadership and race are co-constructed in schools, school systems, and other educational settings (Schein, 1992). Yet in educational leadership we see so much research that ignores these social forces that one wonders whether we have missed some of the most important factors and variables entirely.

It seems clear that this conceptual ambiguity is also a barrier to improved leadership in schools. At DuBois, teachers and administrators had no common language with which to have a discussion about race and racism. This was in part because of the subcultures and cultures in the community, and likely also because there was no administrator or teacher willing to bridge the rift between the Black and White leadership subcultures in the school. There are many outstanding books, articles, and programs to help educators and students discuss race (e.g., Pollock, 2006; Singleton, 2006; Singleton & Linton, 2006; Tatum, 2007). Importantly, this research also shows that there is a silent *and* a spoken language of racism. Increasing one's awareness of race and discussing issues with peers is only the beginning—we must endeavor to interrogate and reflect on our implicit and explicit behaviors to develop a deeper understanding of racism and the myriad ways it influences educational leadership. Still, awareness of attitudes and behaviors is not enough. Heightening awareness by reading books like this one and many others cited on these pages is a start. But awareness must be followed by understanding—through the examination of both quantitative and qualitative data in an educational leader's immediate context. This in turn leads to developing intent, which entails a plan for action. At a school like DuBois this plan might include formal strategies such as book circles or professional development, but it also might include informal strategies like individual educators bringing up issues in the hallways or at lunch. Actions, of course, should follow, and then there should be time devoted to reflection on processes and outcomes. This cycle should take into account personal, professional, and scholarly histories and experiences (see Figure 9.1). Importantly, the cycle is recursive and ongoing.

Race Occurs Simultaneously in Multiple and Ever-Changing Historical, Social, Political, and Economic Contexts

Race is a multilevel phenomenon, and these levels interact with one another in a fluid manner (Scheurich & Young, 1997). While we can gain some insight by reading contemporary studies and histories of race,

Figure 9.1. Moving from Awareness to Understanding, Intent, Action, and Reflection on Issues of Educational Leadership and Racism

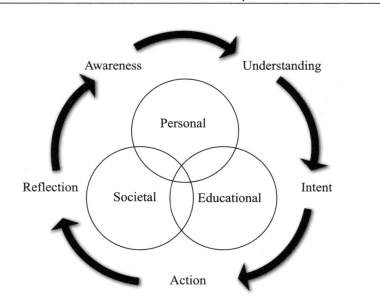

racism, and race relations that look at national-level dynamics or through federal law, we also must be aware that there are 50 state-level histories of race; thousands of county, municipality, and city histories of race; regional differences in race; and tens of thousands of family, neighborhood, and community histories of race that are equally important. Likewise, each school district, school, college, university, educational leadership preparation program, and international organization such as the National Educational Association (NEA), the American Association of School Administrators (AASA), UCEA, and AERA has a history of race. Moreover, each individual—*you, and every person in your life*—has a personal history of race that began a long time ago and is still not finished but will continue throughout the person's lifespan.

Each of these histories has psychological, social, political, and economic dimensions (Brooks & Normore, 2005; Brown, Davis, & McClendon, 1999). These dynamics and histories are constantly evolving and exerting reciprocal influence on one another. That is, each individual's personal race history is in *some* ways intertwined with these other racial dynamics and is in *other* ways an intensely personal and subjective experience. This should urge educational leaders, and the people who prepare and train them, to consider how personal history shapes their perspectives and actions in the context of other histories (Brooks & Tooms, 2008). Leaders must seek to develop an understanding of how they can and do influence the collective and individual experiences of their fellow educators and students in their charge. This perspective—that race is both a subjective personal experience and a multilevel social phenomenon—also should prompt educational leaders to develop a greater awareness of racial issues within and between people and subcultures within their organizations and communities. We simply cannot presume that we "understand race" because we have experienced, read, or researched the topic—race and racism are manifest in different ways everywhere we go and evolve over time at individual, institutional, and societal levels simultaneously.

Interestingly, at DuBois High School, several teachers and administrators had reflected on issues of race, but few actively sought to learn more about race, racism, and education beyond their personal experience. Even fewer felt they had any agency to engage issues of race and racism in any other way than acting as an isolated individual. Many felt, with some justification, that it was dangerous to bring up issues of race, which precluded the possibility of anti-racism as a school-wide value or movement. There are barriers and facilitators with regard to racism at every level of educational leadership; true leaders seek to identify them, and true leadership is the creation of new strategies that positively influence the experiences of students and educators in their schools and systems.

By Omission or Commission, We Are All Engaging Issues of Race

Race is not the specialized domain of activists, the "leadership for social justice crowd," or teachers, administrators, scholars, and graduate students of color. It is instead an issue for *all* educational leadership scholars and practitioners, like it or not. To illustrate this point, I suggest a typology of racial engagement. In doing so I contend both that (a) there are many ways to engage and ignore issues of race, and (b) the way we engage and ignore these issues often varies from situation to situation, and when we interact with different people at different times. Consider the ways in which you, your colleagues, and your organizations might assume one or a combination of these roles in different aspects of your leadership practices:

- *The Apathetic Role.* Has some awareness and knowledge of racial issues, but does not speak out or act on this awareness.
- *The Absolvist Role.* Believes that race is not his/her problem. Absolvists may believe that they live in a racially homogeneous community, leave the work to others because it is too difficult, or simply be ignorant of racial dynamics. But, as we are part of a fluid global community and racial issues permeate all levels of society, the idea that engaging racial issues "is someone else's job" is misguided.
- *The Alchemist Role.* Insists that lead is gold. Alchemists' attitude toward issues of race is based on a false assumption that what they have always done is tantamount to social justice. This often is based on the "irrefutable proof" that they once had a student of color who graduated or that they "treat all students the same way, regardless of race."
- *The Ally Role.* Works with others for racial equity behind the scenes.
- *The Advocate Role.* Urges others to change their behavior, mostly on behalf of other people rather than for their personal gain.
- *The Activist Role.* Opposes or supports a position through vigorous deeds and proactive work, often in a highly visible manner.
- *The Anti-Racist Role.* Develops and implements practices that actively fight racism at the interpersonal and organizational levels. Anti-racists seek to dismantle hegemony and eradicate oppression in their personal and professional work.

At DuBois, teachers and administrators assumed primarily the alchemist and absolvist roles. This was a school where educators believed that issues of race and racism were there, but either not their problem or a problem beyond their power to influence. This meant that hardly anyone was engaging the issues. Now, I turn attention to several issues related to research.

Research That Ignores Issues of Race Is Bad Science

In an era of inquiry marked by widespread assertions that "scientifically based" research is superior to "nonscientific" research, it is curious that quite a lot of so-called "scientifically based" research ignores issues of race. Ignoring a phenomenon *every* social science has acknowledged as an important and powerful social force is to selectively omit pertinent information that likely has either a direct or an indirect influence on the subject(s) of interest. Color-blind research, and probably more generally difference-blind research (Larson & Murtadha, 2002), is simply bad social science, and we as a field have far too much bad science. While one may be able to espouse an insular logic that allows for the "control" of race as a phenotypic variable, it is impossible to control for fluid social dynamics that take many overt and covert forms, change from situation to situation, and evolve over time. Moreover, consider that an increasing body of research contends that administrators and teachers have a tremendous influence over school culture (Brooks & Miles, 2010). Coupled with the fact that these educators are more mobile than at any time in the nation's history, it stands to reason that school cultures fluctuate wildly as teacher and administrator attrition rates continue to climb. Researchers must seek to understand and account for the multiple ways in which race and racism manifest as individual dispositions, but also as organizational phenomena, and "other ways in which [they] function in society" (López, 2003, p. 69). This will demand increasingly sophisticated mixed-method research, in addition to increased historical and philosophical inquiry. Narrowing the scope of what constitutes valid and useful research in the direction of prejudicing one method or approach over a proliferation of methods and approaches not only defies common sense, but is bad science that ignores the protean nature of education, schools, and leadership.

Finally, this research showed that not only are race and racism crucial to understanding educational leadership, but so too is understanding intersectionality [see *Journal of School Leadership, 18*(2) for more about intersectionality], that is, understanding the way that complex ecologies of social forces such as race exert reciprocal influence on one another. It is important to understand how racism, sexism, ableism, ageism, and so on influence one another.

Failing to Include Racial Dynamics in Educational Leadership Research Will Render the Field Obsolete, and Already Has Left It Woefully Incomplete

Although I have strong personal convictions related to the issue, I make this point *not* as a political activist with a "liberal" agenda, but as a social scientist. While there are many ways to conceptualize "leadership" as a research phenomenon, scholars commonly define it as the art and science of influencing a group of people toward a common goal (Northouse, 2010; Yukl, 1998). If we accept this as a broad-brush definition, it follows that studies of leadership must take into account social forces that compromise or privilege certain people's and/or groups' ability to exert influence—and we must include the study of *who* is influenced and how. Race, as a culturally constructed instrument of oppression, has tremendous impact on individual and organizational leadership, precisely because it privileges some and constrains others. While the relatively paltry amount of educational leadership research on race may or may not be a moral disgrace—in terms of what it suggests about the field's commitment to providing equitable schools for all students—it *does* indicate that the knowledge base that undergirds the study and teaching of educational leadership fails to consider important social dynamics of influence, the very subject scholars in the field purport to "understand" in their research.

It is important for *all* researchers to consider race because it is a critical aspect of the study of influence—it is the intellectual responsibility of educational leadership scholars to investigate race, as well as the other social forces mentioned in this chapter. However, although I make this point while supposedly "setting aside moral arguments," competent and caring social scientists will place moral sensitivity at the forefront of their consciousness and methodological orientation when conducting research (López & Parker, 2002). The results of color-blind research can have, and have had, dire consequences for children and adults alike, and contribute to the establishment of ideologies that "developed to justify slavery" (Darling-Hammond, 1995, p. 340), which led to the promulgation of eugenics as a viable epistemology for research (Selden, 1999), and which have led to misinformed public policy and debate over inherent "shortcomings" of people based on race (Darling-Hammond, 1995).

Research as the master's whip? Oppression, indeed. Educational leadership in particular, as a field, has a long history of advancing racist research ideologies via a "conspiracy of silence" (Blount, 1998), by failing to take account of issues of difference in general, and issues of race in particular (Young & Laible, 2000). This issue is further compounded by a proliferation of euphemistic terms such as *social justice, diversity,* and *equity* that are useful to a point but that allow people—particularly people who oppress and enjoy uncritical forms of privilege—to ignore more concrete and difficult dynamics such as racism, sexism, ageism, and ableism. How do YOU engage and ignore various issues of race in educational leadership? It's a question we should all consider.

While Issues of Race Are Important for Everyone, White Men in Particular Must Engage Issues of Race and Race Relations in Educational Leadership

As White men such as myself make up an extremely high proportion of practicing educational administrators and professors of educational leadership, our silence on issues of race speaks volumes. Until White men engage issues of race, and use their disproportionate amount of privilege and power for equity rather than to perpetuate hegemony, they are exacerbating the problem. Importantly, silence is not a neutral stance; White men must understand that by neglecting to proactively engage, understand, and interrogate issues of race in their leadership, teaching, service, and research, they are participating in a longstanding tradition of oppression, exclusion, and marginalization in educational leadership (Young & Laible, 2000). White men's collective and historic lack of engagement in issues of race is the "White elephant in the room" of educational leadership, the overwhelming issue about which few will speak (Wynne, 1999).

While it is important for anyone in education to do so, it is particularly important for White men to actively seek to unlearn our miseducation about race, leadership, and the relationship between them. We cannot be content with color-blind or difference-blind decisions, datasets, and assumptions. Leaving our assumptions and behaviors unexamined will leave us with what we have had in the United States for some time, and that status quo has meant inequitable educational processes and outcomes for people of color. Once we raise our awareness, consider our agency, and commit ourselves to being a force for equity rather than a force for oppression, we have begun to take a step in the right direction. Importantly, however, I do not advocate for a White-Men-as-Savior model of leadership. It is important that White men who lead listen first, support and advocate for underrepresented and oppressed peoples, and, using their privilege, create opportunities for others. Self-aggrandizement and self-promotion are a form of oppression that will only lead us back to another form of White privilege.

CONCLUSION

I don't pretend to be an expert on issues of race in educational leadership, but I do count them among the most important issues facing the field today and I am committed to learning more about and studying these dynamics in my own teaching, service, and research. I am personally committed, morally and intellectually, to understanding and trying to teach about and conduct inquiry on leadership, broadly conceived, and this demands an investigation and interrogation of issues that affect influence, such as race. I acknowledge that many similar arguments can be made for issues of gender, sexual orientation, class, and so on. Yet as a White male professor conducting social science-based inquiry on educational leadership, I feel it is both my intellectual and moral responsibility to explore these dynamics. I hope you will find that this book helps you to consider your own attitudes, beliefs, and behaviors on race and educational leadership—regardless of your race—and to amend this work with your own. I also hope that you are or become a catalyst for issues of race in educational leadership through your teaching, service, and research.

The Myth of a
Post-Racial Society—
A Conversation with Bill Ayers

I first met Bill Ayers at a qualitative research conference in St. Louis when I was a graduate student. I loved his passion, advocacy stance toward issues of justice, manner of presentation, and the fact that he urged the audience, largely graduate students in education, to read the work of sociologists and anthropologists. Better yet, he told us we should all read Studs Terkel's work if we wanted to understand qualitative inquiry.

This conversation, which I recorded with Bill as he announced his retirement from the University of Illinois–Chicago, explored the changing landscape of education and racism in the Obama era.

BROOKS: What initial reaction do you have about race, race relations, and racism in schools?

AYERS: One of the things that mark the moment we are living through is this insistent idea that we are beyond race. Our country was built on White supremacy and it's flourished on White supremacy. White supremacy is absolutely one of the most entrenched but durable features of our national identity. Even as it changes colors somewhat and even as it changes meaning through the centuries, White supremacy finds a way to reassert itself as a dominant cornerstone of what our society looks like. If you think about it, the challenge to White supremacy in the 18th century was the Atlantic slave trade. The challenge in the 19th century was slavery. The challenge in the 20th century was civil rights and the end of apartheid. Here we are again. The challenge today is the criminal justice system. In each of those eras, common sense said there was no way to change it or end it. In each of those eras, people found ways not only to mount a challenge to the reality before them, but to win significant victories. Also, in each of those eras, White supremacy came roaring back in a new start.

So, it blows my mind, frankly, being 65 years old, to look back
at the past 40 years when we mounted a giant, almost irresistible
campaign against Jim Crow and apartheid with the first public
debilitations which seemed to be victorious and seemed to be
overcome. And yet, you look around 40 years later and say, "Oh
my god . . . there is a group of people living much as their great-
grandparents lived." But instead of the cause being race and racism,
it is now a criminal justice system that is far from being color-blind.
It is color-coded. That to me speaks volumes about the tenacity of
the demon known as White supremacy. How does this play out in
schools? It plays out in schools because we see that all of the kinds of
advantages that some kids get are denied to large numbers of poor,
immigrant, working people, and particularly the descendants of
African slaves. We end up with a school system that in a democracy is
indefensible. A school system that has in the same geographic location
a school that educates its kids at $30,000 to $40,000 per kid per year.
That is a crude measure of the kind of resources put in one school
and 4 miles down the road is a school that educates its kids on less
than $4,000 per year. And here is no surprise . . . the kids in the public
school are the kids of color, kids whose forbearers were enslaved
people or who were immigrants from third-world countries. So this is
the state of our union right here.

Even in a system like Chicago or New York, where you have really
excellent public schools standing a few miles away from a crumbling
public school, and you would say, "The formula must be the same
for these two neighboring public schools." But what you lose in that
vision is that the school that is succeeding is raising private money at
an astronomical rate. My granddaughter goes to a school in New York
City that we call a public school plus. It is in neighborhood where
the parents are all professionals or they are artists or are in the arts.
Even if it's not entirely White, it is to some degree. All of the parents
are from privilege. They raised last year close to a quarter of a million
dollars for after-school programs, teachers' aides, Saturday school,
clubs, games, sports, art, a poet in residence, a drama teacher, a clay
studio. Beautiful, except it has nothing to do with equity. It has to
do with carrying your privilege with you. But then worse than that
is, there was a punk piece in the *New Yorker* about Arne Duncan and
it was a typical *New Yorker* profile, you know—loving and fawning
and a beautiful photograph. It pointed out that the University of
Chicago laboratory schools, Arne Duncan's alma mater, and where
the Obama kids went when they lived in Chicago and where also my
kids went, have a cap on classroom enrollment at 15. Fifteen. You find

well-resourced classrooms with a respected and unionized teacher corps. Unionized. You find a curriculum based on pursuing children's interests. Now if that is good enough for Arne Duncan and the Obama kids, then why aren't we touting that as a standard which we want to approach for all of our children in this democracy?

Instead the standard is test score, test score, test score. That would never be the standard for Arne Duncan's kids or the President's kids. So when they moved to Washington, DC, and the press speculated where the girls would go to school, there was never a doubt in my mind that they wouldn't go to Sidwell Friends, which is where they go. And what did they find there? Well-resourced classrooms, a cap at 15, unionized teachers, a well-respected school. If it is good for those kids, then in a democracy, it should be the standard we are trying to achieve for all of the kids in Washington, DC, or the west side of Chicago. Not that we will achieve it tomorrow, but that is what our goal is. To say anything less would be to destroy any idea that we could have a democracy, a real democracy, as opposed to a formal and fake democracy. That is the state of things in my view. It is hard for me to wrap my mind around what rationale or explanation could have a standard anything less than that, but our attention is taken with test scores, ACT scores, and all of the rest of the trophies that are meant to, in my view, take us away from the reality of what we should be aspiring to. The claim that we are living in a post-racial world and we are past the civil rights movement, it seems to me to be a cover for the problems that have reasserted themselves. We are quite a long, long, long way from right racial reconciliation, racial justice, or participatory democracy or a fair and democratic society. How about that for an opening?

BROOKS: You touch on one issue in particular that really came out in the study of DuBois. I saw a lot of what Joel Spring and some other people call second-generation segregation, where you see segregation within schools by programs, basically tracking. All of the remedial types of classes are full of Black faces. All of the AP classes are full of White faces.

AYERS: It is a good phrase because under the guise that we are all mixed up in here together, who gets the better kids? Who gets the kids that are consistently misbehaving? What about detentions? What about suspensions and expulsions? In Chicago, the suspension/expulsion rate for Black boys is quadruple that of Whites. It is just unbelievable. How do you explain that? Well, the explanation is that they behave badly. That's also the explanation for why Black men go to prison at the rate they do. There is nothing about it that is justifiable, fair, or defensible. Yet, that is the world we live in.

BROOKS: One of the themes that came out of the study is "expel to excel." The school systematically expelled African American students, supposedly for behavior problems. But I sat in rooms where they would talk about it and it was really because these students were doing poorly on state tests and it was going to count against the school. They were looking for any kind way, any loophole not to count them and include their scores.

AYERS: This is one of the things I think is really, really important. You remember the Texas Miracle? The Texas Miracle was a fraud from top to bottom. I will give you one example of a turnaround school. Orr High School in Chicago has been turned around. You wouldn't believe it, but their test scores have gone up, up, up in the past year. You look at it and you say, "Man, that is really incredible. How did they do that?" You look a little closer and you realize that the kids taking the exam last year were in their junior year in high school. This year, though, you had to be a "certified junior" to take the test. To be certified, you had to have a passing grade in all of your classes, which means they tested half the kids this year. Surprise! The test scores went up. That's how these people manipulate it.

The other astonishing thing is when reformers like you say, "Look, we can make a good urban school. We can do it right here, right now. All we need is these kinds of resources, this type of commitment, and a little, hate to say it, intelligence applied to the situation." So you do that. But they say, no, no, Jeff. You're faking it. You're looking at things like attendance and bios. We're not into that. We want test scores. They say your program is bullshit and that they are going to do it their way. Then they do it their way and they come up with Harlem Children Zone or they come up with high school, the Green Dot High School in Los Angeles. And they say, "Look at this. In 2 years, look what we have accomplished." Sure enough they have done some good things in both of those places. In Harlem they have done some good things because Jeff Cannon is a lovely and charismatic person. A hard-working person is able to raise literally millions of dollars from private foundations. The Green Dot School in L.A. has literally millions of private dollars. There was the story in *The New York Times* last week about this Green Dot School that used to be a haven for gangs and drugs and rape and violence and now it is much, much better. Deep in the article in *The New York Times* it says that the test scores haven't moved but they have better attendance, less violence, less graffiti, and less suicide. God bless them. I'm all for that. I think that is great. But they did that with millions of extra resources not provided by the community or government, but by private donations—and the test scores are not better because of it. Then they say we ought to repeat this Harlem Children's Zone all over the country, yet without the money. That is insane.

BROOKS: I am going to shift the focus a little bit here. One of the things that emerged from the study was the way that this urban school was portrayed in the media.

AYERS: One event that comes to mind is a basketball game that I attended. It was, to be honest, one of those almost dream-like sort of events that you hope kids will be a part of when they are in high school. The gym was filled with a community that was enthusiastically supporting the team. There was one photographer from the local paper that zeroed in on one tiny incident. I was there the whole time and didn't even know it happened. The next morning, there was this article about gang activity at the school and how the basketball games were a cover for other stuff. It was just totally baseless, crazy, negative stuff. It really struck me how consistently this type of negative portrayal is used to describe underperforming or urban city schools. When you go to the schools, there are some tough circumstances but you see some great stuff happening too.

Assumptions do go on and it is so insane. The *New Yorker*, the bastion of liberalness, does a feature called the Rubber Room. It is a longer form journalism like a typical mini-ethnography. It takes place in a room in a Central Office where teachers that have been judged too messed up to be in a classroom are waiting for their cases to be adjudicated through the contract. It is a fascinating article. I read it with absolute lip-smacking satisfaction. These people are actually crazy, you know. These people are really some misfits and some nut cases. So it is fun to read. It is about six teachers in a system of 40 to 50 thousand teachers. You hear the state drum beating in the background . . . get rid of the lazy, incompetent teachers. They aren't lazy and incompetent. During the 2008 election John McCain would say we have to get rid of the lazy, incompetent teachers. What am I going to do? Stand up and say, "No, no, no. The lazy and incompetent must stay for my granddaughter?" Everybody agrees with that. But, if I can change the frame, if I could get to the microphone first, I would say every public school kid deserves an intellectually curious, morally competent, ethical, compassionate, caring, well-rested, and well-paid teacher in the classroom. You can't go to a city in this country without having some form of that *New Yorker* article be a part of a feature article in the newspaper. If you go to L.A. or St. Louis, you will see some teacher that is kept on because of a union contact. I think you can say it is really crazy.

BROOKS: Another thing that came out was that the demographics of the school were basically about 85 to 90% Black students and about 15% White students. The teaching population was about 50% White to 50% Black. One of the things I saw over and over, especially talking to White teachers, was an uncritical sense of White privilege. It came out especially in their teaching. There was a lot of culturally irrelevant pedagogy. There was a lot of flat-out cultural abuse. There was no conversation about race going on in the school. There was nothing to prompt these teachers and administrators to question their assumptions about language and about the way people dressed, what people ate, the cars they drove, and how they looked, at all of that.

AYERS: This is the result of the pretense of being beyond race, which gives permission to reassert White supremacy without shame, without doubt, without any sense that there is another way to look at this same issue. Amanda Lewis's book *Race on the Playground* is the same kind of story. Where people unabashedly put forward a White assumption. Amazing.

BROOKS: So many of the teachers rattle off so many of the things you expect to hear from that perspective. For example, "I have one Black friend so I am not racist," and "All kids can learn." Which really means, "I don't have to worry about kids of color and their particular needs."

AYERS: Exactly.

BROOKS: It came to me that there is a real need for leaders and educators in general to unlearn their miseducation about racism and about leadership and to take on deconstructing issues of race. I find in my own experience, and maybe that is too limited, but when I start talking to people about how to do that kind of stuff, their eyes glaze over or they are like, "It's not me." I wonder, just how do we start to talk with educators about taking this apart and looking deeply at themselves and what they are doing in their institutions around race?

AYERS: This is a very complicated question and a very complicated issue. Race and class intermingle in our culture. There is tremendous confusion, which makes us more innocent and naïve but also more complicit. It is the confusing of racism, the ideology, the idea, and the prejudice with White supremacy, the structure, the deep question of privilege and oppression. It's not racism when they say, "Not me," or when they put up their White blind spots. What they are saying is, "I am not personally prejudiced. I actually slept with a Black person." Yet, it is not about their personal prejudice. It's actually about a system that you benefit from as a White person or you suffer from as a Black person without you personally doing anything. You don't have to do anything because the thing bubbles along. So I often, when I am making the argument in my classes, I often tell people that I find it easier for women sometimes to understand a couple of examples. One example is when I was first teaching at UIC, this figure of a university, my classes would get out at 8 o'clock at night on the near east side of Chicago. Men just left class and scattered to the train, the bus, and the parking lot. The women congregated together and went out together. It took me a couple of months to notice that. Why would I notice? I am not bonding together. I finally asked someone, "Why are you bonding together? Is it because you feel safer?" Of course, stupid. Of course. "We can't go out there all by ourselves at 8 o'clock at night right here, right now." Well, once I saw it, I announced it and we talked about it in class and it became an example of male privilege. Unearned, unasked for, not wanted, but nonetheless there it was. You could say, "I'm not sexist." Good for you. But what are you doing about the fact that women are required to approach the leaving of class differently than you are because you are given the privilege of gender? People tend to get an example like that. It's not about you personally. It's not about you being a mean or bad person. It is structured into the realities that we live with. Then the question is, "Can we as a group of men bond together with a group of women and fight that oppression and privilege? Can we find ways?" And the answer is yes. But to say this as an analogy for White people—it's not that you yourself did something, you just happened to benefit from the way things are.

The other example of course is heart-wrenching, and is a bigger reach for people. We all have American privilege, every one of us. We live in a country that has not been a field of battle in the past 40, 50, 100 years. We have not suffered the wounds of war on our territory. Another example of American privilege is that 4% of the U.S. population consumes 25% of the world's energy, taking it for granted and then getting all excited about the fact that there is such a thing called foreign oil. What the hell is foreign oil? Who invented that racist concept? Privilege does not have to do with our personal values or necessarily your experiences. It has to do with the structures that are bigger than you and have been in place long before you. That is what we have to find a way to oppose.

BROOKS: There is a line in a Charles Bukowski poem that comes to mind. One of the problems with American people is that their houses have never been bombed.

AYERS: Exactly. When I am talking to a group of Black and White students or just Black students, I will often make the point of American privilege because it is too easy to say, "Oh, woe is me. I miss the fact that we all enjoy a certain privilege." Now, someone like me who is 65 years old, White, and male grew up in enormous privilege in terms of wealth. Plus, those things are easy to identify. But everyone is enjoying certain things at the expense of other people. The point of knowing that is not to make ourselves crazy with guilt. The point of knowing that is to give us a map toward action. Seeing the reality and being astonished by it require us to do something. That is the point of it.

BROOKS: You talked about White supremacy, and that being linked to power. Power is very closely connected to this notion of leadership, administration, and management. What is your perspective on school leaders, principals, and superintendents?

AYERS: The models that we are borrowing from are professional models from business schools. In my view this doesn't fit well with education because education in a democracy is based on the idea that every human being is of incalculable value. That every student is also a potential teacher and every teacher is also a learner. Every leader is also a follower. And so on. The leadership and management notions that interest me the most are horizontal and not vertical, are collective and not individual. Yet we live in a culture and society that is so driven by the notions of the free market, individual entrepreneurship, and individualism. But, what is public and what is private? What has always been competitive? Since 1980 the dollarization of the private sector and the dollarization of the market and the demonization of the public have been so, so profound and so weighted. It might even become the case that the word *public* is racially coded. When we say public housing, public hospital, public transportation, and public welfare, we are talking about Black people. I mean that is astonishing, when you stop and think about it. But that is how far we have come, when the very idea of public is an idea of Black people. Oppositely, the idea of the private is the shiny-faced, Princeton graduate who is off making a new business. Privatizing the public schools is one of the few places there is money still to be made. You know I am adverse to the notions of leadership that are individual and heroic and White and male. I just returned from the U.S. Social Forum where I spent a week. While there I saw 20,000 activists who were young and primarily of color. It was something to rejoice in. The idea that we don't have to think vertically but that we can share horizontally and build something much stronger in the long run.

BROOKS: The census projections to 2050 show that the United States is going to look very different over the next several decades.

AYERS: I don't think there is any question about that. Forty years ago the great James Baldwin said that America is no longer White and will never be White again. That was a long time ago and it is truer every year. The idea of these panicked dislocated folks who see their solution, their salvation in building a wall and keeping out the Brown people are so sadly misdirected. It is true that in 2050 the country will be different from today. I think the other thing we ought to remind ourselves about is the world of 2050 will be what we make of it. Capitalism and imperialism is in its death throes. I don't think there are any questions about it. All of the indicators are there. I mean, if you were running Spain, what would you do? Would you cut all of the social services, which they did, and turn around and still get a rotten bond rating? I mean, what is the solution? They are doomed. The reason they are doomed is the trajectory of consume, consume, consume, growth, growth, growth has an end. You can't go on forever. So here we are living in a real sustained crisis. A depression, but the depression is not in and of itself the crisis. The crisis is the long-term decline. Saying it is going to come to an end in no way suggests that the system we will have in 2050 or say 2100 is going to be better than what we have today. It could be far worse. It could be much more vicious, and if you think about, the move from feudalism to capitalism was a costly move in terms of human suffering even though it was progressive in terms of its direction. The move from capitalism to whatever is next is also going to be costly. At what cost is going to depend on what people open their eyes to, recognize, and so forth. What we are seeing of course are people in a panic, not knowing what to do, hyperpatriotism, new kinds of racism, genocidal schemes. All of this stuff is on the agenda—new forms of slavery. It really requires that people who want to stand up for humanity and the possibility of a humane world have their work cut out for them. There is no doubt about that.

BROOKS: There is an Anna Wren quote that says there can never be a final victory over oppression; we will always reform and come at you from another angle.

AYERS: Absolutely. I have given up on the idea there is going to be a perfect world. I think that is pure utopianism and a little bit foolish. But what we can do is fight for more egalitarianism and more democracy. That is what we should be fighting for. I think a lot of the left spends its time plotting out the world, the socialist world we are going to beget. Yet they are missing a screw or something. Can you imagine before the French Revolution people, most feudalist and the emerging middle class, recognized that feudalism was done? Scrambling to try and figure out what was next? None of them could have predicted the institutions that would be put into place to create capitalism. That was something that was worked out as they went along. I think it is a waste of time to try and figure out what socialism will look like when we don't have any idea if we are going to have socialism. It is much more important to fight on the side of humanity against the kinds of crushing blows that we are getting in privatizing everything and incarcerating everyone in sight. We have to fight these things. We have to fight these things very, very seriously.

BROOKS: Where is the battleground? Is it local? Is it through research? Is it through trying to influence policy? What is your take?

AYERS: The wonderful and yet terrible thing is that the battleground is everywhere. That means if you are a researcher there is surely stuff to be done. If you want to know where I think the large-scale battles are going to take place, one of those places is education. What kind of education are we going to have and where are we going to get that education? Another battleground is going to be how we figure out how to live a sustainable life. That is a local struggle with a global perspective. I like the slogan fight locally, think globally. I think that is a smart thing to say. If you look at the struggles in Detroit, or the struggles in the Southwest, or the struggles in Chicago, you can see that both labor and environmental concerns are connected with the issues of peace and justice. These things do fit together, perfectly in some ways. I think we have to recognize that there is no perfect place to struggle. Never has been. Never will be. Therefore, that too can be a waste of energy to figure out where the vanguard is located. Where do I need to be? Be where you are. Fight where you are. Make the connection. Do two things simultaneously. One is to reframe the debate. Constantly fight to get rid of the clichés that are the dominant metaphors that control our lives. Reframe the debate and then connect whatever you are doing with others. I fight in education but I connect education to labor, demonization of queers, to the oppression of peace in the world, and global justice. I mean the idea, for example, that we are laying off 300,000 teachers and we are not allowed to raise the question, "By the way government . . . what about that trillion-dollar military budget . . . can we have just a fraction of it?" It would solve the budget crisis in a minute. You can't talk about it because somehow war is not your issue. You're in education.

That is why Martin Luther King was such a genius as an activist. He rejected all of his advisers that told him that the war in Vietnam was not his issue. His response to them was to say, "If you don't think that is my issue, then you don't understand me and you don't understand what the issues are because the war in Vietnam is very much my issue." That is the way it is today. We have to make these three or four wars, endless wars, that the U.S. is conducting, a point of struggle. We have to recognize that the only growth industry we've got is killing and war and surveillance and incarceration. We have to fight it. We have to say hire teachers. Hire social workers. Get rid of the military. We don't want recruitment on our campuses. We don't want the ROTC. We don't want our military. Get rid of it. Abolish the prisons. I could go on.

BROOKS: In the past few years several influential books have come out about educators as activists. When I visit schools, I see a few people talking about that kind of work and doing those kinds of things, standing up to apathy, indifference, and avoidance of the issues.

AYERS: Well, there is nothing new in that. When I was an organizer for Students for a Democratic Society, I drove from campus to campus at the height of the 1960s. At every campus people would say that everyone is apathetic here. I was at the University of Michigan and the people at Michigan would say, "I wish I was at Columbia where they are really active." And then you go to Columbia and they would say why can't we be like Paris where they are tearing down a government. Well, hey, why don't you just get over yourself, you know. You are where you are. You live where you live. The important thing is to find a way to open your eyes not once or twice but every day in every way to look at the injustices. Act on what you see and understand and then rethink. To me, the rhythm of being an activist never changes. Open your eyes. Act. Doubt. Open your eyes again. Act again. Doubt again. That is what it means to be an activist. Apathy is the common place where most of us won't do anything. That's part of the challenge. In other words, I used to say to people when I traveled for SDS, they would tell me how fucked up their campus was and I would always say back to people, "Now you just described for me reality as you see it. Even assuming you are right, all that does is tells you the conditions under which you have to make a plan of organizing. You haven't just told me therefore to do nothing. So we have to do something."

BROOKS: Right, absolutely. One of the things I want to finish off with is, What would you like to see happening in schools that isn't happening right now?

AYERS: Well, I actually think that schools, in some ways schools, are proxying for society in general. That is to say, if you were to ask, "How do you change schools?" I could give you an easy kind of silver bullet, linchpin-type answer, but I would be way off. I would be missing a lot.

Just like if you had said, How do you change society because changing the schools is as complicated as changing society? That is why I am willing to take anyone that is not making a profit off of kids—anyone, Geoff Canada, the Green Dot School, as well as teachers' unions, anyone else. I am willing to say everyone can play a role. Everyone can play a part. Where I get off your train, though, is when you say my project is the only project that works. I don't buy that. Charter schools can play a role in the rejuvenation and struggle ahead. Unions can play a role. Reform projects can play a role. There are a lot of people that can play a role. But as soon as you say, Teach for America is God's gift to the world and that is what is going to change the world, then I think you are an idiot. What I would say if you were to say to me, "What if you were Arne Duncan?" What if I were Arne Duncan? Well, first of all I would have to shoot myself and after that I would organize a series of campaigns. In Chicago I would like a campaign that says this is our city. This is our education. It would be a mobilization of a vast Vesey, a democratic community assembly organized explicitly to draw on the wisdom of everyone in order to rethink and renew curriculum and teaching. I hate the fact that in Washington a bunch of professional pinheads think they know better than the people of Chicago what would make good curriculum and teaching. I want a vast Vesey, a democratic assembly throughout the country everywhere. I would start a second campaign. A massive initiative centered on bringing parents and unemployed folks into the schools. It wouldn't be that expensive. Imagine if every classroom in the west side of Chicago had two parents and an unemployed person helping out. That would make my day.

The third campaign would be for pure, restorative justice. Get rid of the three strikes and you are out law. Get rid of zero tolerance. Instead build in every school and in every community creative spaces for long reflections and teachable moments. I would have a big campaign to take any profit and any privatization out of the public space. I would end high-stakes testing. I would lead a massive movement to redesign assessment in the service of kids and for the service of teachers. Not to judge which one is going forward and which one is not. I would have a massive campaign to end segregation based on race, class, ability, status, background, which really means equal access to funding. So if Winnetka Public Schools can raise $40,000 per kid per year for expenditures, then I want that to be the standard for every kid. Lastly, I would demilitarize the schools and go over to the Pentagon and say no more recruitment in city schools. You can recruit in any other ways you want to but you cannot go into our schools. That is how I would begin changing the schools.

Methodological Appendix

This appendix is a brief overview of issues related to the research design, data collection techniques, data analysis procedures, and ways I established rigor in the process.

RESEARCH DESIGN

As this research was an investigation of racism and educational leadership practice from a cultural perspective, I employed an ethnographic research design (Creswell, 1998). The study took place in a public high school in the southeastern United States, referred to throughout this book as the pseudonymous DuBois High School. The student demographic distribution at the school is 85% African American and 12% White (with 3% listed as "Other"). This case study, which took place in a single urban high school over the course of 2 academic years, explored various aspects of the topic of interest, from a variety of theoretical perspectives that evolved over time. After an initial pilot study that focused on social justice (see Chapter 2), the following broad research question guided all inquiry:

How does racism influence the practice of educational leadership?

DATA COLLECTION

Data were collected via interviews, observations, and technical and non-technical documents (Silverman, 2001). I gained initial access to the school through an assistant principal who introduced me to teachers, administrators, and other educators throughout the duration of the study. While this gatekeeper was helpful at the onset, I used snowball sampling to recruit other participants into the study so that I would be able to gain multiple perspectives from educators who might be outside the immediate social network of this administrator. Teachers and administrators largely accommodated my requests for interviews and were amenable to my presence as I observed their meetings and intimate work with students and colleagues. Over the course of 2 academic years, I conducted a total of 105 formal interviews with 52 different teachers and administrators, each of which lasted between 45 minutes and 2 hours. During many of the 452 observation hours I logged during the 2 years, I also engaged in numerous informal interviews. Some technical documents, such as the School Improvement Plan and an accreditation report, were freely accessible public documents. I collected other technical documents, such as discipline plans, meeting agendas, and memos, whenever available. Primary nontechnical documents such as posters in classrooms, notes, and email messages also were collected or reproduced with participants' consent.

DATA ANALYSIS

Data were analyzed using an analytic induction coding process (Patton, 2002). I began with broad conceptual categories based on the theoretical perspective at hand, and then within these categories I began open coding, which was used as a preliminary technique to "break open" the data and suggest more refined themes. The resultant open codes then were combined with other conceptually similar open codes to form axial codes. Axial codes then were collected into particular categories, which then were developed into the themes presented in this book (see Figure A.1).

As suggested by Strauss and Corbin (1998), speculative or tentative analysis during data collection served to further sharpen certain foci of the study, helped reveal insights, and stimulated further pursuit of certain aspects of the literature. As additional data were analyzed, categories were refined and then developed into the emergent, then substantive, themes presented in this book.

VALIDITY

As a means of establishing internal validity, I conducted systematic and ongoing member checks with teachers and administrators throughout the duration of the study (Silverman, 2001). During these checks, participants offered their assessment of the accuracy of interpretations of the themes and findings. In nearly every instance, member checks urged the researchers to explore and refine themes further; at no point did a participant suggest that analyses were incorrect. Findings presented in this book were consistent with both researchers' interpretations and members' perspectives.

Figure A.1. Research Process

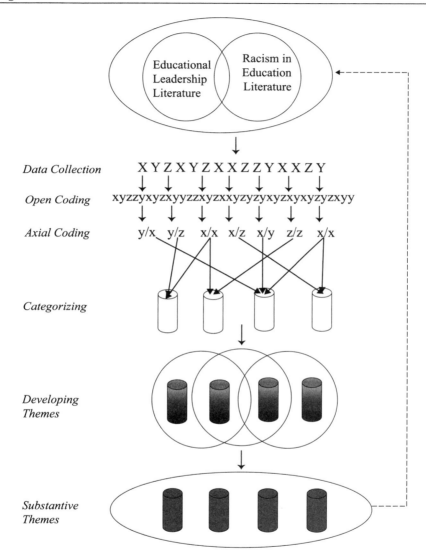

In this figure, uppercase X = interviews (primary field data), Y = observations (primary field data), and Z = documents (primary field data); lowercase x, y, and z represent coded data derived from primary field data; axial codes are shown as y/x, etc. Initial categories are depicted by clear cylinders, but as they become saturated with data, their color deepens.

References

Alston, J. (1999). Climbing hills and mountains: Black females making it to the superintendency. In C. C. Brunner (Ed.), *Sacred dreams: Women and the superintendency* (pp. 79–90). Albany: State University of New York Press.

Apple, M. W. (1990). *The hidden curriculum and the nature of conflict in ideology and curriculum.* New York: Routledge.

Apple, M. W. (1995). *Education and power.* New York: Routledge.

Apple, M. W. (1996). *Cultural politics and education.* London: Open University Press.

Blount, J. M. (1998). *Destined to rule the schools: Women and the superintendency, 1873–1995.* Albany: State University of New York Press.

Bogdan, R. C., & Biklen, S. K. (1998). *Qualitative research for education: An introduction to theory and methods.* Boston: Allyn & Bacon.

Bogotch, I., Beachum, F., Blount, J., Brooks, J. S., & English, F. W. (Eds.). (2008). *Radicalizing educational leadership: Toward a theory of social justice.* Rotterdam, Netherlands: Sense Publishers.

Brooks, J. S., & Normore, A. H. (2005). An Aristotelian framework for the development of ethical leadership. *Journal of Values and Ethics in Educational Administration, 3*(2), 1–8.

Brooks, J. S. (2006a). *The dark side of school reform: Teaching in the space between reality and utopia.* Lanham, MD: Rowman & Littlefield Education.

Brooks, J. S. (2006b, April). *Educational leadership and justice: An interdisciplinary perspective.* Paper presented at the annual meeting of the American Educational Research Association, San Francisco.

Brooks, J. S. (2006c). Tinkering toward utopia or stuck in a rut? School reform implementation at Wintervalley High. *Journal of School Leadership, 16*(3), 240–265.

Brooks, J. S. (2007, Summer). Race and educational leadership: Conversation catalysts to prompt reflection, discussion, and action for individuals and organizations. *UCEA Review, XLVII*(2), 1–3.

Brooks, J. S. (2008). Introduction. In I. Bogotch, F. Beachum, J. Blount, J. S. Brooks, & F. W. English (Eds.), *Radicalizing educational leadership: Toward a theory of social justice* (pp. 1–16). Rotterdam, Netherlands: Sense Publishers.

Brooks, J. S., & Jean-Marie, G. (2007). Black leadership, white leadership: Race and race relations in an urban high school. *Journal of Educational Administration, 45*(6), 756–768.

Brooks, J. S., & Kensler, L. A. W. (2011). Distributed leadership and democratic community. In F. W. English (Ed.), *The Sage handbook of educational leadership: Advances in theory, research, and practice* (2nd ed., pp. 55–66). Thousand Oaks, CA: Sage.

Brooks, J. S., & Miles, M. T. (2006). From scientific management to social justice . . . and back again? Pedagogical shifts in educational leadership. *International Electronic Journal for Leadership in Learning.* Available at http://www.ucalgary.ca/~iejll/

Brooks, J. S., & Miles, M. T. (2010). The social and cultural dynamics of school leadership: Classic concepts and cutting-edge possibilities. In S. D. Horsford (Ed.), *New perspectives in educational leadership: Exploring social, political, and community contexts and meaning* (pp. 7–28). New York: Peter Lang Publishing.

Brooks, J. S., Scribner, J. P., & Eferakorho, J. (2004). Teacher leadership in the context of whole school reform. *Journal of School Leadership, 14*(3), 242–265.

Brooks, J. S., & Tooms, A. K. (2008). A dialectic of social justice: Learning to lead through reflection and dialogue. *Journal of School Leadership, 18*(2), 134–163.

Brown, F. (2005). African Americans and school leadership: An introduction. *Educational Administration Quarterly, 41*(4), 585–590.

Brown, M. C., Davis, G. L., & McClendon, S. A. (1999). Mentoring graduate students of color: Myths, models, and modes. *Peabody Journal of Education, 74*(2), 105–118.

Bryant, N. (1998). Reducing the relational distance between actors: A case study in school reform. *Urban Education, 33*, 34–49.

Camburn, E., Rowan, B., & Taylor, J. E. (2003). Distributed leadership in schools: The case of elementary schools adopting comprehensive school reform models. *Educational Evaluation and Policy Analysis, 25*, 347–373.

Capper, C. A. (Ed.). (1993). *Educational administration in a pluralistic society.* Albany: State University of New York Press.

Cohen, R. L. (1986). *Justice: Views from the social sciences.* New York: Plenum.

Collins, P. H. (2009). *Another kind of public education: Race, schools, the media, and democratic possibilities.* Boston: Beacon.

Conley, D. (2000). *Honky.* Berkeley: University of California Press.

Creswell, J. W. (1998). *Qualitative inquiry and research design: Choosing among five traditions.* Thousand Oaks, CA: Sage.

Dantley, M. E. (2005). Faith-based leadership: Ancient rhythms or new management. *International Journal of Qualitative Studies in Education, 18*(1), 3–19.

Dantley, M. E., & Tillman, L. C. (2006). Social justice and moral transformative leadership. In C. Marshall & M. Oliva (Eds.), *Leadership for social justice: Making revolutions in education* (pp. 16–30). Boston: Pearson Education.

Darling-Hammond, L. (1995). Cracks in the bell curve: How education matters. *The Journal of Negro Education, 64*(3), 340–353.

Deal, T. E., & Peterson, K. D. (1999). *Shaping school culture: The heart of leadership.*

San Francisco, CA: Jossey-Bass.

Delpit, L. (1995). *Other people's children: Cultural conflict in the classroom.* New York: New Press.

Donaldson, G. A. (2006). *Cultivating leadership in schools: Connecting people, purpose and practice.* New York: Teachers College Press.

English, F. W. (2005, November). *Towards a theory of social justice/injustice: Learning to lead in the social cage.* Paper presented at the annual convention of the University Council for Educational Administration, Nashville.

Evans, S. W., Axelrod, J., & Langberg, J. M. (2004). Efficacy of a school-based treatment program for middle school youth with ADHD: Pilot data. *Behavior Modification, 28*(4), 528–547.

Fluehr-Lobban, C. (2006). *Race and racism: An introduction.* Lanham, MD: AltaMira Press.

Fordham, S. (1996). *Blacked out: Dilemmas of race, identity, and success at Capital High.* Chicago: University of Chicago Press.

Fordham, S., & Ogbu, J. (1986). Black students' school success: Coping with the burden of "acting white." *The Urban Review, 18*(3), 176–206.

Freire, P. (1989). *Pedagogy of the oppressed.* New York: Continuum.

Fullan, M. (2001). *Leading in a culture of change.* San Francisco: Jossey-Bass.

Furman, G. C. (2004). The ethic of community. *Journal of Educational Administration, 42*(2), 215–235.

Gay, G. (1997). Multicultural infusion in teacher education: Foundations and applications. *Peabody Journal of Education, 72*(1), 150–177.

Giroux, H. A. (1988). *Teachers as intellectuals: Toward a critical pedagogy of learning.* Westport, CT: Bergin & Garvey.

Goldstein, J. (2004). Making sense of distributed leadership: The case of peer assistance and review. *Educational Evaluation and Policy Analysis, 26*(2), 173–197.

Gooden, M. A. (2005). The role of an African American principal in an urban information technology high school. *Educational Administration Quarterly, 10*(4), 630–650.

Grogan, M. (1999). Equity/equality issues of gender, race, and class. *Educational Administration Quarterly, 35*(4), 518–536.

Hacker, A. (2003). *Two nations: Black and white, separate, hostile, unequal.* New York: Scribner.

Hall, E. T. (1959). *The silent language.* New York: Doubleday.

Hall, E. T. (1966). *The hidden dimension.* New York: Doubleday.

Hall, E. T. (1968). Proxemics. *Current Anthropology, 9*(2-3), 83–107.

Hall, E. T. (1977). *Beyond culture.* New York: Doubleday.

Hall, E. T. (1984). *The dance of life.* Garden City, NY: Anchor Press/Doubleday.

Hargreaves, A. (1993). Individualism and individuality: Reinterpreting the teacher culture. In J. W. Little & M. W. McLaughlin (Eds.), *Teachers' work: Individuals, colleagues, and contexts* (pp. 51–76). New York: Teachers College Press.

Horsford, S. D. (2010). Mixed feelings about mixed schools: Superintendents on the complex legacy of school desegregation. *Educational Administration Quarterly, 46*(3), 287–321.

Jackson, B. L. (1988). Education from a black perspective: Implications for leadership preparation. In D. E. Griffiths, R. T. Stout, & R. B. Forsyth (Eds.), *Leaders for America's schools: The report and papers of the National Commission on Excellence in Educational Administration* (pp. 305–316). Berkeley, CA: McCutchan.

Jazzar, M., & Algozzine, B. (2007). *Keys to successful 21st century educational leadership.* Boston: Pearson Education.

Jean-Marie, G. (2006, Winter-Spring). Welcoming the unwelcomed: A social justice imperative of African-American female leaders. *Educational Foundations, 20*(1-2), 83–102.

Jean-Marie, G., & Normore, A. H. (2006). A repository of hope for social justice: Black women leaders at historically black colleges and universities. *International Electronic Journal for Leadership in Learning, 10*(20). Available at http://www.ucalgary.ca/~iejll

Johnston, C. (1997). *Leadership and learning organisation in self-managing schools.* Unpublished Ed.D thesis, University of Melbourne.

Ladson-Billings, G. (1992). Liberatory consequences of literacy: A case of culturally relevant instruction for African American students. *The Journal of Negro Education, 61*(3), 378–391.

Ladson-Billings, G. (1995a). But that's just good teaching! The case for culturally relevant pedagogy. *Theory into Practice, 34*(3), 159–165.

Ladson-Billings, G. J. (1995b). Toward a critical race theory of education. *Teachers College Record, 97,* 47–68.

Ladson-Billings, G. J. (1995c). Toward a theory of culturally relevant pedagogy. *American Education Research Journal, 35,* 465–491.

Ladson-Billings, G. J. (1997). *The dreamkeepers: Successful teachers of African-American children.* San Francisco: Jossey-Bass.

Ladson-Billings, G. J. (1998). Teaching in dangerous times: Culturally relevant approaches to teacher assessment. *The Journal of Negro Education, 67*(3), 255–267.

Lambert, L., Walker, D., Zimmerman, D. P., Cooper, J. E., Lambert, M. D., Gardner, M. E., & Slack, P. J. F. (1995). *The constructivist leader.* New York: Teachers College Press.

Lankshear, C. (1993). Functional literacy from a Freirean point of view. In P. McLaren & P. Leonard (Eds.), *Paulo Freire: A critical encounter* (pp. 90–118). New York: Routledge.

Larson, C. L., & Murtadha, K. (2002). Leadership for social justice. In J. Murphy (Ed.), *The educational leadership challenge: Redefining leadership for the 21st century* (pp. 134–161). Chicago: University of Chicago Press.

Lee, S. S., & McKerrow, K. (2005, Fall). Advancing social justice: Women's work. *Advancing Women in Leadership Online Journal, 19,* 1–2. Available at http://

www.advancingwomen.com/awl/fall2005/preface.html

López, G. R. (2003). The (racially neutral) politics of education: A critical race theory perspective. *Educational Administration Quarterly, 39*, 68–94.

López, G. R., & Parker, L. (Eds.). (2002). *Interrogating racism in qualitative research methodology*. New York: Peter Lang.

Lortie, D. C. (1975). *Schoolteacher: A sociological study*. Chicago: University of Chicago Press.

Marshall, C., & Gerstl-Pepin, C. (2005). *Re-framing educational politics for social justice*. Boston: Allyn & Bacon.

Marshall, C., & Oliva, M. (Eds.). (2006). *Leadership for social justice: Making revolutions in education*. Boston: Pearson Education.

Marshall, C., & Young, M. (2006). The wider societal challenge. In C. Marshall & M. Olivia (Eds.), *Leadership for social justice* (pp. 307–319). Boston: Pearson.

Maxcy, B. D., & Nguyen, T. S. (2006). The politics of distributing leadership: Reconsidering leadership distribution in two Texas elementary schools. *Educational Policy, 20*(1), 163–196.

McLaren, P. (1993). *Schooling as a ritual performance*. New York: Routledge.

McLaren, P., & Torres, R. (1999). Racism and multicultural education: Rethinking "race" and "whiteness" in late capitalism. In S. May (Ed.), *Critical multiculturalism: Rethinking multicultural and antiracist education* (pp. 42–76). London: Falmer Press.

Merchant, B. M., & Shoho, A. R. (2006). Bridge people: Civic and educational leaders for social justice. In C. Marshall & M. Oliva (Eds.), *Leadership for social justice: Making revolutions in education* (pp. 85–109). Boston: Pearson Education.

Mitra, D. (2006). Student voice or empowerment? Examining the role of school-based youth–adult partnerships as an avenue toward focusing on social justice. *International Electronic Journal for Leadership in Learning, 10*(22). Available at http://www.ucalgary.ca/~iejll

National Center for Education Statistics. (2007). *Digest of education statistics 2007*. Washington, DC: U.S. Department of Education.

Northouse, P. G. (2010). *Leadership: Theory and practice* (5th ed.). Los Angeles: Sage.

Ogbu, J. (1978). *Minority education and caste: The American system in cross-cultural perspective*. San Diego, CA: Academic Press.

Patton, J. M. (1998). The disproportionate representation of African Americans in special education: Looking behind the curtain for understanding and solutions. *Journal of Special Education, 31*, 26–33.

Patton, M. Q. (2002). *Qualitative research and evaluation methods* (3rd ed.). Thousand Oaks, CA: Sage.

Pearson, S. B., & Newcomb, M. D. (2000). Predictors of early high school dropout: A test of five theories. *Journal of Educational Psychology, 92*(3), 568–582.

Perry, T., Steele, C., & Hilliard, A. I. (2003). *Young, gifted and black: Promoting high achievement among African-American students*. Boston: Beacon.

Pollock, M. (2006). Everyday antiracism in education. *Anthropology News*, 47(2), 9–10.

Postman, N., & Weingartner, C. (2000). *Teaching as a subversive activity*. New York: Dell.

Pounder, D. G., Ogawa, R. T., & Adams, E. A. (1995). Leadership as an organization-wide phenomenon: Its impact on school performance. *Educational Administration Quarterly, 31*, 564–588.

Quick, P., & Normore, A. H. (2004). Moral leadership in the 21st century: Everyone is watching—especially the students. *The Educational Forum, 68*(4), 336–347.

Sawicki, J. (1991). *Disciplining Foucault: Feminism, power, and the body*. New York: Routledge, Chapman and Hall.

Schein, E. H. (1992). *Organizational culture and leadership* (2nd ed.). San Francisco: Jossey-Bass.

Scheurich, J. J. (2002). *Anti-racist scholarship: An advocacy*. Albany: State University of New York Press.

Scheurich, J. J., & Skrla, L. (2003). *Leadership for equity and excellence: Creating high-achievement classrooms, schools, and districts*. Thousand Oaks, CA: Corwin.

Scheurich, J. J., & Young, M. D. (1997). Coloring epistemologies: Are our research epistemologies racially biased? *Educational Researcher, 26*(4), 4–16.

Schusky, E. L. (1972). *Manual for kinship analysis*. New York: Holt, Rinehart, and Winston.

Selden, S. (1999). *Inheriting shame: The story of eugenics and racism in America*. New York: Teachers College Press.

Senge, P. M. (1990). *The fifth discipline: The art and practice of the learning organization*. New York: Doubleday/Currency.

Sernak, K. (2006). School reform and Freire's methodology of *conscientization*. *International Electronic Journal for Leadership in Learning, 10*(25). Available at http://www.ucalgary.ca/~iejll

Shapiro, J. P., & Stefkovich, J. A. (2001). *Ethical leadership and decision making in education*. Mahwah, NJ: Lawrence Erlbaum Associates.

Shoho, A. R., Merchant, B. M., & Lugg, C. A. (2005). Social justice: Seeking a common language. In F. English (Ed.), *The Sage handbook of educational leadership: Advances in theory, research, and practice* (pp. 47–67). Thousand Oaks, CA: Sage Publications.

Silverman, D. (2001). *Interpreting qualitative data: Methods for analysing talk, text and interaction*. London: Sage.

Singleton, G. E. (2006, March). "Breaking the silence": Ushering in courageous conversations about the impact of race on student achievement. Presentation to the Los Angeles Unified School District. Available at www.pacificeducationalgroup.com/Breaking%20the%20Silence%20LAUSD.pdf

Singleton, G. E., & Linton, C. (2006). *Courageous conversations about race: A field guide for achieving equity in schools*. Thousand Oaks, CA: Corwin.

Spillane, J. P. (1999). State and local government relations in the era of standards-based reform: Standards, state policy instruments, and local instructional policy making. *Educational Policy 13*(4), 546–573.

Spillane, J. P. (2005). Primary school leadership practice: How the subject matters. *School Leadership and Management, 25*(4), 383–397.

Spillane, J. P. (2006). *Distributed leadership.* San Francisco: Wiley.

Spillane, J. P., Diamond, J. B., Burch, P., Hallett, T., Jita, L., & Zoltners, J. (2002). Managing in the middle: School leaders and the enactment of accountability policy. *Educational Policy, 16*(5), 731–762.

Spillane, J. P., Halverson, R., & Diamond, J. B. (2004). Investigating school leadership practice: A distributed perspective. *Educational Researcher, 30*(3), 23–28.

Spring, J. (2006). *American education* (12th ed.). Boston: McGraw-Hill.

Starratt, R. J. (1997). Administering ethical schools. In J. Beck, J. Murphy, & Associates (Eds.), *Ethics in educational leadership programs: Emerging models* (pp. 95–108). Columbia, MO: University Council on Educational Administration.

Starratt, R. J. (2004). *Ethical leadership.* San Francisco: Jossey-Bass.

Strauss, A., & Corbin, J. (1998). *Basics of qualitative research: Grounded theory procedures and techniques.* Newbury Park, CA: Sage.

Strizek, G. A., Pittsonberger, J. L., Riordan, K. E., Lyter, D. M., & Orlofsky, G. F. (2006). *Characteristics of schools, districts, teachers, principals, and school libraries in the United States: 2003–04 schools and staffing survey.* Washington, DC: National Center for Education Statistics.

Tatum, B. D. (1999). *Why are all the Black kids sitting together in the cafeteria? And other conversations about race* (2nd ed.). New York: Basic Books.

Tatum, B. D. (2007). *Can we talk about race?* Boston: Beacon.

Terkel, S. (1992). *Race: How Blacks and Whites think and feel about the American obsession.* New York: The New Press.

Tillman, L. C. (2002). The impact of diversity in educational administration. In G. Perreault & F. Lunenburg (Eds.), *The changing world of school administration* (pp. 144–156). Lanham, MD: Scarecrow Press.

U.S. Census Bureau. (2001). The white population: 2000 census brief. Available at http://www.census.gov/prod/2001pubs/c2kbr01-4.pdf

U.S. Census Bureau. (2004). Census Bureau projects tripling of Hispanic and Asian populations in 50 years; non-Hispanic whites may drop to half of total population. Available at http://www.census.gov/PressRelease/www/releases/archives/population/001720.html

Valles, E. C. (1998). The disproportionate representation of minority students in special education: Responding to the problem. *Journal of Special Education, 32,* 52–57.

West, C. (1998). *Race matters.* New York: Vintage Books.

Whyte, D. (2001). *Crossing the unknown sea: Work as a pilgrimage of identity.* New York: Riverhead Press.

Wolcott, H. F. (2003). *Teachers versus technocrats*. Walnut Creek, CA: AltaMira Press.

Wynne, J. T. (1999, April). *The elephant in the living room: Racism in school reform*. Paper presented at the annual conference of the American Educational Research Association, Montreal.

Wynne, J. (2003). The elephant in the classroom: Racism and school reform. In R. Duhon-Sells (Ed.), *International perspectives on methods of improving education: Focusing on the quality of diversity* (pp. 58–88). New York: Edwin Mellon Press.

Young, M. D., & Brooks, J. S. (2008). Supporting graduate students of color in educational administration preparation programs: Faculty perspectives on best practices, possibilities, and problems. *Educational Administration Quarterly, 44*(3), 391–423.

Young, M. D., & Laible, J. (2000). White racism, anti-racism, and school leadership preparation. *Journal of School Leadership, 10*(5), 374–415.

Yukl, G. (1998). *Leadership in organizations*. Upper Saddle River, NJ: Prentice-Hall.

Zhang, D., & Katsiyannis, A. (2002). Minority representation in special education: A persistent challenge. *Remedial and Special Education, 23*, 180–187.

Index

Accreditation, 59
Achievement gap, 9, 13, 70
Administration
  team, 24, 29, 42, 95, 102
African-American, 68
  superintendents, 38
Ambiguity, 34, 55
Antithesis, 38, 39, 45
Assimilation, 31
Attrition, 27
Ayers, William, 4, 125–136

Banking education, 23
Barriers, 28, 34, 51
Behavior, 101
  avoidance, 101, 104
  incompetence, 101, 104
  indifference and apathy, 101,
    104–106, 135
  unethical, 101–102, 107
Beliefs, 38
Black churches, 29
Bridge people, 22, 28, 34
Bridgework, 29, 30, 35
Brown v. Board of Education, 73
Budget, 25
  misappropriation of, 77–78, 103
  and private donations, 128, 136
Buzzwords, 103

Camaraderie, 42, 46
Care, 63–64
Change, 26, 105

Code-shifting, 45, 93
Communication, 28, 29, 46, 55, 89–91
Community
  beliefs, 43, 68
  Black, 86
  division, 70
  goals, 33
  leadership, 33
  linkages, 29, 97
  outreach programs, 30
Complementarity, 38, 39, 45
Comprehensive school reform, 20
Conley, Dalton, 51
Counter narrative, 71
Critical activism, 32, 35
Critical consciousness
  (*conscientizacão*), 23, 30, 34
Critical dialogue, 25, 32
Cronyism, 102, 107
Cultural capital, 30
Cultural communication, 91
  association, 93
  avoidance of, 106
  body language, 91–92
  defense, 99
  hierarchy, 93
  interaction, 90–91
  learning, 97
  play, 98
  sexuality, 95
  subsistence, 94
  temporality, 96–97
  territoriality, 95

Culturally irrelevant pedagogy, 130
Culture(s)
  Black, 46, 52
  Black education, 59
  of disadvantage, 44, 52, 53
  interaction among, 39, 67
  lack of Black, 60, 68, 70, 94
  of mistrust, 47, 110
  mores of, 91
  norms, 37–38, 91, 94
  school, 37, 121
  school and community, 31, 33, 43,
      55, 94
  subcultures, 37–39
  two different subcultures, 45, 97
  values, 42, 52–53, 68
  White, 46, 54, 55
  White subculture, 42
Curriculum, 54–56, 104

Data, 55, 82–83, 106
Dialogue, 33, 34, 36, 78, 84
Discourse, 27
Distributed critical activism, 30
Distributed leadership, 17, 18, 32, 34,
    35
Distrust, 45
Duncan, Arne, 126, 136

Ethics, 38
Extracurricular events, 104

Freire, Paulo, 21, 23, 34
Frustration, 29, 54, 55, 63

Gangs, 82
Gender, 40, 95, 131
  Black men, 68, 109
  gender roles, 41, 43, 95, 109
  White women, 43, 131
Giroux, Henry, 22
Gooden, Mark, 38

Good ol' boys network, 43, 44, 108
Guidance counselor, 41, 61
  as advocate, 41
  as role model, 41

Hall, Edward, 89–91
Hegemony, 17, 23
Hidden curriculum, 26, 74, 89
Hierarchy, 96
Homosexuals, 40
Honky (Conley), 51

Institutional knowledge, 27
Institutional racism, 74, 79, 88, 130
Institutional rewards, 43
Instruction, 103
International Baccalaureate (IB), 13,
    26, 27, 31, 34, 73–75, 83
  Black students and, 79–81, 86
  diversity and, 81, 86
  multicultural and, 81
  principal and, 77–78, 81–82, 86
  racism and, 78–79, 87
Intersectionality, 121

Jean-Marie, Gaetane, 3, 33
Jokes, 99

Language, 67
Leadership
  accountability, 101–102
  anti-intellectual, 25
  Black, 38, 40–42, 78, 95
  Black women, 40–41, 95
  collaboration (with stakeholders),
      33
  critical activists, 23–24, 32, 34
  democratic, 38
  difference-blind, 18, 121, 123
  fluidity in, 35
  followers, 19–20
  formal, 20, 34, 45

hierarchy of, 42, 95, 96
individual bridgework, 29
informal, 20, 25, 34, 41, 45
instructional, 104
for liberation, 25
male-dominated (patriarchal),
    42–43
minority, 38
misleadership, 101–102, 123
non-verbal, 100
practice, 18–19, 38, 123
preparation, 35–36
race, 117, 123
respect, 42–43
routines, 19–20
situations, 19–20
social justice, 21, 23, 123
trust, 33
vision, 43
White, 39–40, 42–44, 95, 123
Leaderspeak, 45
Learning, 97–98, 104
Lortie, Dan, 99
Lying, 110

Media, 129
Meetings, 54, 55, 59
Moiety, 3, 37–39, 45–46
Morality, 122
    moral compass, 40–41, 95

National Merit Award, 105
Normore, Anthony, 3, 33
Norms, 31, 38, 46, 83

Obama, President Barack, 126–127
Oppression, 22, 87

Parents, 63
Physical space, 96
    divided among racial lines, 96
Policies, 31, 34, 41, 101

Political capital, 32
Politics
    formal, 27
    informal, 25
Post-racial, 125, 127
Power, 51, 95
    female, 43
    male, 43
Principal(s)
    accountability, 107
    activism, 41
    attrition of, 121
    Black, xiii, 10, 12, 27, 34, 41–42, 44,
        46, 78
    care, 70
    communication, 29, 35, 42, 45–46
    delegating, 106–107
    fatigue of, 104, 106
    incompetence, 104
    mentoring, 42
    mismanagement, 77, 102
    professional dress, 28, 41–42, 85
    professionalism, 106
    racism in, 82
    recruitment of teachers, 42, 44
    social class of, 82
    stress on, 106
    White, 45–46
Principal-teacher disconnect, 57, 74
Procedures, 31, 101
Professional development, 98
Public intellectualism, 24, 27

Race, 5, 44, 46, 51, 69, 78, 86
    allegiance to, 47, 68, 70, 98, 103
    culturally constructed, 117, 122
    difference, 67, 74, 81, 99
    diversity, 37, 79
    division, 13, 42, 46, 73, 98–99
    history of, 118–119
    influence of, 122
    informal association, 93, 99

Race *(continued)*
  phenotype, 5, 10, 87, 116
  relations, 37–38, 40, 42, 46, 67–68,
    71, 98
  sociological construct, 87
  stereotypes, 44, 53, 55, 57, 81, 94
  trust, 110
Racial engagement, 120
Racial segregation, 73
Racial solidarity, 93
Racialized closed door autonomy, 99
Racialized instruction, 89
Racially biased assessment, 89
Racism, 1, 6, 26, 45–46, 52–53, 55, 60,
    71, 78, 115
  acting White, 81, 88
  anti-racism, 38, 119
  Black, 83
  Black-on-Black, 70, 81, 92
  Black-on-White, 82
  body language, 91
  communication, 89, 93, 100, 117
  dialogue, 83, 117
  discrimination, 116–117
  prejudice, 116
  White, 38, 42, 52, 68, 73, 83
  White-on-Black, 82, 91–92
Reading coach, 54
Reciprocity, 38–39, 45
Rewards, 63, 102
Rivalry, 38, 39, 45, 98
Routines, 29, 35

Schein, Edgar, 38
School grades, 54, 71
School Improvement Plan, 46, 59, 75,
    97, 103
School standards, 55
Second-generation segregation,
    73–74, 79, 127
Sernak, Kathy 23
Sexual harassment, 107–110

Silence, 46, 67, 89, 93, 117, 123
Social class, 46, 51, 81
  Black elitism, 81–82
  lower class, 46
Social justice, 3, 17–18, 21
  activism for, 31, 34, 40–41, 135
  awareness of, 23, 28, 35
  bridge people, 22, 28
  bridgework, 30
  equity, 22, 30–31, 33, 38
  inequity, 28, 116
  leadership, 23
  marginalization, 22–23
  obstacles, 22, 28
  oppression, 23, 26, 87, 116–117
Spillane, James, 17, 20
Student(s)
  accountability, 60, 68
  achievement, 43, 44, 57, 65, 68, 70,
    75–76, 82
  behavior, 53, 56, 63, 127–128
  Black, 43, 52, 56, 66, 71, 74–75, 79,
    81
  clothing, 52, 65, 84
  college, 30, 65–66, 69, 76, 83
  discipline, 60
  expectations, 68, 71, 74
  failure, 52–53, 55–56, 57, 59–60, 63,
    70–71
  family influence on, 43–44, 52, 57
  fear, 64
  homosexual (gay), 41
  inequity, 30, 74
  interrelationships, 33
  job skills, 30, 53, 55
  marginalized, 34, 71
  names, 104, 105
  opportunities, 44, 57, 65, 67, 74
  poverty, 44, 57, 67
  race, 28, 43, 56, 68, 71, 74, 84
  success, 68, 76, 85
  support, 30, 44, 46, 53, 57, 69, 85

testing, 53, 55, 71, 76, 82, 127–128
trust, 69
values, 43, 46, 52, 70–71

Tea Party, vi
Teacher(s)
  activism, 31, 62, 78
  anger, 57, 59, 83–84
  attrition, 83, 101, 105, 121
  Black, 42, 86, 98, 102
  communication, 65, 68–69
  cultural differences, 12, 44, 52–53, 57
  discipline, 56
  diversity, 31, 79
  dress, 85–86
  engagement, 69, 71
  evaluations, 57–58, 107
  experience, 64
  family, 66
  frustration, 110
  honesty, 65, 83
  incompetence, 102
  influence, 64, 69
  isolation, 55, 57, 59, 68, 104
  lack of community, 58, 63–64
  license, 25, 102
  lounge, 27
  mentoring, 42, 63
  modeling, 53
  neophyte, 27, 58
  noncompliance, 54, 86, 102

pay, 13, 69, 77
professionalism, 69
racial differences, 10, 13, 52–53
racism, 56
responsibility, 55–56, 69, 85
as role model, 68, 69, 85
sacrifices, 66
stress, 52
student motivation, 53, 63–65
success, 56, 62, 85
teacher-leaders, 24, 26, 31, 42–43
transformational public
    intellectuals, 25–26, 34–35
tutoring, 85
veteran, 27, 42, 43, 69
White, 98
work ethic, 62, 103
Teacher-student relationships, 69, 82
Tension, 25
Time, 19, 30, 52, 96–97
Traditions, 13, 98
Transactional, 45
Transformational practices, 45–47

Underground economy of
    instructional resources, 96

White privilege, 38, 44, 51, 71, 74, 83,
    115, 123
White supremacy, 125–126, 130
Wolcott, Harry, 37, 39

About the Author

Jeffrey S. Brooks is Associate Professor and Program Coordinator of Educational Administration at Iowa State University. His research focuses on sociocultural and equity dynamics of educational leadership practice and preparation, and his most recent work examines how globalization and racism influence leadership in schools. Dr. Brooks has conducted case study and ethnographic research in the United States and in the Philippines, where he studied leadership for social justice as a J. William Fulbright Scholar. He is author of *The Dark Side of School Reform: Teaching in the Space Between Reality and Utopia* and co-editor of the forthcoming edited volumes *Instructional Leadership for Social Justice: What Every Principal Needs to Know in Order to Lead Equitable and Excellent Schools* (with George Theoharis) and *Educational Leadership and Racism: Preparation, Pedagogy and Practice* (with Noelle Witherspoon Arnold). Dr. Brooks' work has appeared in many peer-reviewed educational research journals. He is Editor of the *Journal of School Leadership* and Series Editor of Information Age Publishing's *Educational Leadership for Social Justice* book series.